CAMPAIGN 355

MALPLAQUET 1709

Marlborough's Bloodiest Battle

SIMON MACDOWALL   ILLUSTRATED BY GRAHAM TURNER
Series editor Marcus Cowper

OSPREY PUBLISHING
Bloomsbury Publishing Plc
Kemp House, Chawley Park, Oxford OX2 9PH, UK
1385 Broadway, 5th Floor, New York, NY 10018, USA
29 Earlsfort Terrace, Dublin 2, Ireland
www.ospreypublishing.com

OSPREY is a trademark of Osprey Publishing

First published in Great Britain in 2020

© Osprey Publishing, 2020 – Email: info@ospreypublishing.com

A catalogue record for this book is available from the British Library.

ISBN: PB 9781472841230; eBook 9781472841247; ePDF 9781472841216;
XML 9781472841223

21 22 23 24 25   10 9 8 7 6 5 4 3 2

Maps by bounford.com
3D BEVs by Paul Kime
Index by Zoe Ross
Typeset by PDQ Digital Media Solutions, Bungay, UK
Printed and bound by Bell & Bain Ltd., Glasgow G46 7UQ

Artist's note

Readers may care to note that the original paintings from which the colour
plates in this book were prepared are available for private sale. All
reproduction copyright whatsoever is retained by the publishers. All
enquiries should be addressed to:

Graham Turner, PO Box 568, Aylesbury, Bucks. HP17 8ZX UK
www.studio88.co.uk

The publishers regret that they can enter into no correspondence upon
this matter.

Note on photographic images

Unless otherwise indicated, the images that appear in this work are from
the author's collection.

The author and publishers wish to thank the Musée d'Histoire Militaire
(Military History Museum), Tournal for permitting the use of several images
in this work. The museum is located at Rue Roc Saint-Nicaise 59–61, 7500
Tournai, Belgium, and contains numerous rooms dedicated to Tournai's
military history from 1100 up to 1945.

Osprey Publishing supports the Woodland Trust, the UK's leading woodland
conservation charity.

To find out more about our authors and books visit
www.ospreypublishing.com. Here you will find extracts, author
interviews, details of forthcoming events and the option to sign up for
our newsletter.

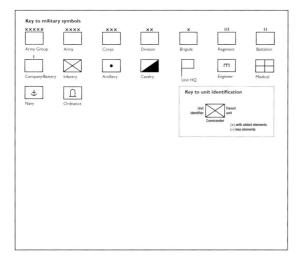

PREVIOUS PAGE
Marlborough and Eugene meet on the edge of the Bois de Sars
during the Battle of Malplaquet. (Painting by Louis Laguerre)

CONTENTS

Western Europe at the outbreak of the War of the Spanish Succession

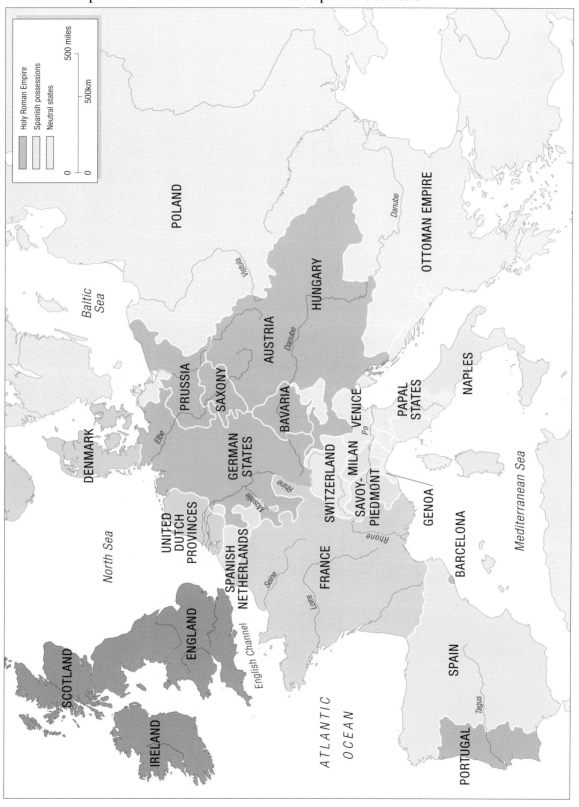

Holy Roman Empire
Spanish possessions
Neutral states

500 miles
500km

POLAND

Baltic Sea

HUNGARY

AUSTRIA

PRUSSIA
SAXONY

DENMARK

BAVARIA

VENICE

Vistula

Danube

Danube

OTTOMAN EMPIRE

PAPAL STATES

NAPLES

GERMAN STATES

Elbe

SWITZERLAND

MILAN

SAVOY-
PIEDMONT

GENOA

Po

Rhine

Moselle

UNITED DUTCH PROVINCES

North Sea

SPANISH NETHERLANDS

FRANCE

Rhone

BARCELONA

Mediterranean Sea

Seine

Loire

SCOTLAND

ENGLAND

English Channel

IRELAND

ATLANTIC OCEAN

SPAIN

Tagus

PORTUGAL

ORIGINS OF THE CAMPAIGN

Malplaquet was the bloodiest battle of the 18th century. On 11 September 1709, hundreds of thousands of men from all over Europe fought over a few kilometres of ground across the modern Franco-Belgian border, resulting in close to 35,000 casualties. The scale of the slaughter shocked Europe. With frontal assaults on entrenched positions, preceded by massed artillery bombardments, Malplaquet was more like the Western Front in 1914–18 than a typical 18th-century engagement.

How did it come to this?

By the end of the 17th century, Louis XIV's glittering court at Versailles led the world in almost everything from fashion to the art of war. When Carlos II of Spain died without an heir in 1700, his will named Louis XIV's grandson, Philippe d'Anjou, as the next king – Philippe's legitimacy stemming from Louis' marriage to Carlos' sister. There was another candidate to the Spanish throne: Archduke Charles, son of the Holy Roman Emperor Leopold, who had married the late King of Spain's other sister.

A painting by François Gerard depicting the recognition of Louis XIV's grandson as King of Spain on 16 November 1700. This was the main cause of the War of Spanish Succession as, unless stopped, France and Spain would be linked under the same royal dynasty. (Leemage/Corbis via Getty Images)

Detail from a tapestry commemorating Marlborough's and Eugene's victory at Blenheim in 1704. This battle shattered the French army's reputation. (The Picture Art Collection/Alamy)

The idea that Spain and France might be united under the same dynasty, perhaps one day under the same king, was more than the other Western European nations could bear. France was the strongest European power, and Spain controlled a vast empire. Together, they would be an unrivalled superpower. Likewise, France could not stomach a similar link between Spain and the Holy Roman Empire. The latter, centred on modern Austria, incorporated much of central Europe, including most of the small German states.

When diplomacy failed to resolve the issue, the War of the Spanish Succession broke out. The Holy Roman Empire (Austria, Hungary and most of modern Germany) and the Maritime Powers (the Netherlands and England) joined together to oppose the union of the French and Spanish crowns. The Iberian Peninsula was torn apart between pro-French and pro-Austrian factions. Catalonia, along with much of Aragon and Valencia, supported Archduke Charles' claim, as did Portugal. The rest of Spain supported Philippe.

These same nations only had four years of peace when the war broke out. The Treaty of Ryswick ended the Nine Years' War (1688–97) between France and the Grand Alliance of the Dutch Republic, England, Spain and the Holy Roman Empire. It had not ended Louis XIV's vision of creating a European superpower, nor had it given Europe time to fully recover from years of conflict.

By 1709, the nations of Western Europe had been fighting for another eight years. War raged along the Rhine frontier, in northern Italy, Spain and the Spanish Netherlands (modern Belgium). It also spread to the far-flung colonies of the European powers from America to India. All of the combatants were feeling the loss in blood and treasure, France most of all. Assailed on all sides by a multitude of enemies who also controlled the seas, the French economy was in tatters, and her population at breaking point. Her armies, once considered invincible, had suffered a series of humiliating defeats.

A contemporary illustration commemorating the Allied victory at Lille, engraved by Jeremias Wolff. (Anne S.K. Brown Military Collection)

The Imperialists (of the Holy Roman Empire), under the command of Prince Eugene of Savoy, won several victories against the French in Italy early in the war. In 1704, the French crossed the Rhine to link up with their Bavarian allies in an attempt to reach Vienna and knock the Imperialists out of the conflict. This incursion was soundly defeated when John Churchill, the Duke of Marlborough, led an army of the Maritime Powers from Flanders to the Danube to link up with Eugene's Imperialists at the Battle of Blenheim. The myth of French invincibility was broken at Blenheim, and the French army suffered further catastrophic defeats in the Spanish Netherlands at Ramillies (1706) and Oudenarde (1708).

Despite their victories in the field, it was not plain sailing for the Allied powers. Holding together a far-flung alliance of many nations required a huge amount of political effort and acumen. The Dutch government was not keen on offensive

The Low Countries, 1708–09

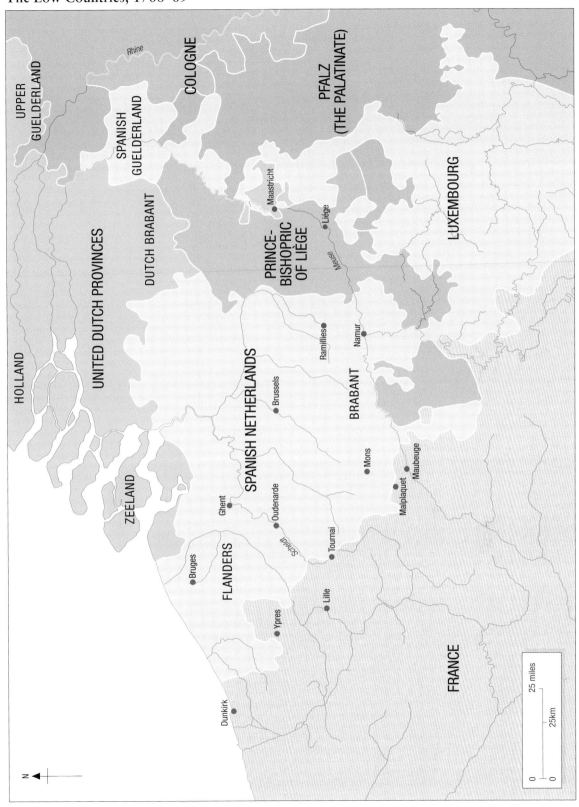

UPPER GUELDERLAND

SPANISH GUELDERLAND

COLOGNE

Rhine

PFALZ (THE PALATINATE)

HOLLAND

UNITED DUTCH PROVINCES

DUTCH BRABANT

Maastricht

Liége

PRINCE-BISHOPRIC OF LIÈGE

LUXEMBOURG

Meuse

ZEELAND

Ramillies

Namur

BRABANT

Brussels

SPANISH NETHERLANDS

Mons

Maubeuge

Bruges

Ghent

Oudenarde

Malplaquet

Scheldt

Tournai

FLANDERS

Ypres

Lille

Dunkirk

FRANCE

N

25 miles

25km

0

0

Marshall Boufflers surrendering the city of Lille to Marlborough in 1708. The victories of that year gave the Allies confidence that they could utterly defeat the French in 1709. (Granger Historical Picture Archive/Alamy)

action that might cost more lives and money than they were prepared to sacrifice. Prussia wanted to be recognized as a kingdom in exchange for its war effort, while Austria was distracted by a Hungarian rebellion and another war between Sweden, Denmark, Saxony, Poland and Russia to the north and east. Marlborough spent as much time in diplomatic shuttling between capitals as he did commanding troops in the field. In this, he was hugely aided by his wife Sarah, who was Queen Anne's favourite at the English court.

After Marlborough's comprehensive victory at Oudenarde and capture of Lille in 1708, the Allies were poised to invade France, and the French were in no state to adequately defend themselves. Although France's frontiers were still intact, most of the fortified towns on the frontier were now in Allied hands, and, except in Spain, the French army had suffered defeat after defeat. After years of war, the French treasury was empty, huge numbers of men had been killed and famine raged throughout the countryside. The situation was so bad that Louis XIV approached the Dutch with a peace offer. The English Lieutenant-General Francis Palmes recorded the French terms as follows:

[The French] made offers to give up Spain, the Indies and Milan to King Charles. [They insisted that Naples and Sicily would go to Philippe.] The Low Countries they were willing to give up … but would not consent to give up Lille, offering Ypres in lieu … The answer [of the Dutch] was that they could not enter into any treaty … that they had treaties with their respective allies and would not give any answer to these proposals, until satisfaction was given to these said treaties.

Although the Allied nations were also sick of war, they felt that they had the upper hand in early 1709. Individual countries sought to gain national objectives through the negotiations. The Dutch wanted a buffer zone of fortified towns between themselves and the French. The English wanted Louis to abandon his support for James Stuart (King James III of England in exile), recognize a Protestant succession to the English throne, to cede Newfoundland and Hudson's Bay and to give England a monopoly over the transatlantic slave trade. All were wary that a union of the Holy Roman Empire with Spain could be as much of a threat to the European balance of power as a union between France and Spain.

The French offer was rejected by the Allies, despite the fact Louis had made concessions on all the points that had caused the war in the first place. Their counter-offer was in turn rejected by the French on 12 June 1709. So, the war continued, resulting in the bloody Battle of Malplaquet three months later.

CHRONOLOGY

1697 The Treaty of Ryswick ends the Nine Years' War between France and the Grand Alliance of England, Spain, the Holy Roman Empire and the Dutch Republic.

1700 King Carlos II of Spain dies, naming Louis XIV's grandson, Philippe d'Anjou, as his heir. The Holy Roman Emperor proclaims his son, Archduke Charles, as King of Spain.

1701 French troops under Louis-François, Duc de Boufflers, occupy the Spanish Netherlands (modern Belgium).

Imperial troops under Eugene move into northern Italy, defeating the French at the Battle of Chiari.

Alliance formed between the Holy Roman Empire, England and the Dutch Republic.

James II of England dies in exile. France recognizes his son as James III.

1702 Death of King William III of England. Ascension of Queen Anne to the throne.

John Churchill given the title of Duke of Marlborough and appointed Captain-General of the Maritime Powers.

Imperial army moves into Pfalz (the Palatinate).

French army commanded by Claude Louis Hector, Duc de Villars, crosses the upper Rhine. Although forced to withdraw, Villars claims victory at the Battle of Friedlingen and is made a marshal of France.

Bavaria sides with France.

1703 The Allies capture Bonn, Kaiserswerth and Liège.

Boufflers replaced by François de Neufville, Duc de Villeroi, to command of the French in Flanders.

Villars' French army breaks through the Black Forest to link up with the Bavarians.

The Franco-Bavarians defeat the Imperialists at Munderkingen and Höchstadt.

Villars resigns his commission when the Bavarians refuse to support an attack on Vienna.

Savoy and Portugal join the alliance against France.

1704 Archduke Charles lands in Portugal to gather support for his claim to the Spanish throne.

Camille d'Hostun, Duc de Tallard, leads French reinforcements into Bavaria.

Marlborough leads an army from the Netherlands to the Danube to link up with the Imperialists and stop the French march on Vienna.

Marlborough and Ludwig Wilhelm von Baden-Baden defeat the Franco-Bavarians at Schellenberg, capturing Donauwörth.

Marlborough and Eugene defeat the Franco-Bavarians at Blenheim.

The English capture Gibraltar.

Bavaria occupied by the Imperialists.

Landau and Trier taken by the Allies.

1705 Marlborough's plan to invade France from the Mosel collapses due to lack of political support.

The French take to the offensive in Flanders.

Marlborough recalled to Flanders from Germany. His plan to counter-attack is thwarted by the Dutch.

French victory over the Imperialists at Cassano in northern Italy.

An Allied army lands in Catalonia, capturing Barcelona.

1706

Marlborough's plan to move his army to Italy to link up with Eugene's Imperialists is vetoed by the Dutch.

French victory over the Imperialists at Calcinato in Italy.

Anglo-Portuguese army occupies Madrid for three months.

Marlborough decisively defeats the French at the Battle of Ramillies.

The Allies take control of most of the Spanish Netherlands.

Eugene's Imperialists relieve the siege of Turin.

France withdraws troops from Italy and the Rhine to reinforce Flanders.

1707

Louis XIV makes peace overtures; these are rejected by the Allies, who quarrel amongst themselves.

Sweden defeats Saxony in the Great Northern War, diverting the emperor's attention to the east. France's attempt to secure an alliance with Sweden fails.

The Acts of Union take effect, uniting Scotland and England as Great Britain.

Allies defeated at Almanza in Spain.

Reinforced from Italy, the French take to the offensive in Flanders. A cat

and mouse campaign ensues, with no major battles.

Eugene invades southern France from Italy. He withdraws after failing to take Toulon.

Political opposition to the war grows in Britain.

1708

Failed French attempt to invade Scotland to restore James III to the throne.

French offensive in Flanders decisively defeated at the Battle of Oudenarde.

Eugene and Marlborough lay siege to Lille, one of the strongest fortresses in Europe.

French attempt to capture an Allied supply convoy for Lille is defeated at Wynendal.

Maximilian II Emanuel, Elector of Bavaria, reinforces the French in Flanders. His attempt to capture Brussels is foiled by Marlborough.

Despite a gallant defence by Marshal Boufflers, Lille falls after a four-month siege.

1709

1 January Ghent and Bruges fall to the Allies.

March Villars appointed to command the army of northern France.

April Louis XIV makes a peace offer which renounces his grandson's claim to the Spanish throne.

17 May Franco-Spanish victory over the Anglo-Portuguese at La Gudina.

28 May After squabbling amongst themselves, the Allies present Louis with a counter-proposal for peace.

May	Villars takes up a strong defensive position on the French frontier with the Spanish Netherlands.
12 June	The Allied counter-proposal is formally rejected by the French.
23 June	Marlborough, reinforced by Eugene, invests Tournai.
7 July	The Allies open siege trenches at Tournai. Villars digs in on the frontier and does not attempt to relieve the town.
3 September	Tournai surrenders.
4 September	Allied advance guard, commanded by the Prince of Hesse-Kassel, advances on Mons.
7 September	Marlborough and Eugene advance on Mons. Villars shifts his position to Malplaquet. Advance guards of the two armies skirmish.
11 September	The Battle of Malplaquet.
15 September	The Allies besiege Mons after the French fall back on Valenciennes and Quesnoy.
20 October	Mons falls to the Allies.
1710	Douai falls to the Allies, but they fail in an attempt to take Arras.
	Allies defeat the French and Spanish at Almenar and Saragossa. They briefly occupy Madrid.
	Decisive French victory in Spain at Brihuega.
	The Tories, opposing the war, win a landslide majority in a British election.
1711	The Holy Roman Emperor Leopold dies. He is succeeded by his son Archduke Charles, who renounces his claim to the Spanish throne.
	Villars constructs a line of fortified defences – the Ne Plus Ultra – in northern France.
	The Allies capture Bouchain in northern France.
	Secret peace negotiations open between Britain and France.
	Marlborough relieved of command and charged with misappropriating public funds.
1712	Britain deserts the Alliance. Eugene appointed to replace Marlborough.
	Villars takes to the offensive. He defeats Eugene at Denain.
	The French recapture Douai, Bouchain and Quesnoy.
1713	The Peace of Utrecht ends the war between France, Spain and the Maritime Powers. Louis XIV's grandson is recognized as Philip (Felipe) V of Spain in return for renouncing any claim to the French throne and recognizing special rights for Catalonia. France retains control of Alsace. Gibraltar, Minorca, Nova Scotia, Newfoundland and Hudson's Bay are ceded to Britain, and France abandons support of the Stuart dynasty. The Dutch gain almost nothing other than an end to the ruinous war.
1714	The treaties of Rastatt and Baden, negotiated between Villars and Eugene, end hostilities between France and the Holy Roman Empire. The Spanish Netherlands, Freiburg, Naples, Milan and Sardinia go to the Holy Roman Empire. In return for imperial recognition of Philip's claim to the Spanish throne, France retains Alsace.

OPPOSING COMMANDERS

THE FRENCH

Claude Louis Hector, Duc de Villars (1653–1734)

Born into the lower ranks of the French nobility in 1651 (his father was a marquis), Villars started his military career in 1671 in the Mousquetaires du Roi. He saw action in the Franco-Dutch War (1672–78) and the Nine Years' War (1688–97). By 1690, he had achieved senior officer rank, serving under Marshal Boufflers in the Ardennes. After the war, he became the French ambassador to Vienna, meeting two of his future opponents: Markgraf Ludwig Wilhelm von Baden-Baden and Prince Eugene of Savoy. When the War of the Spanish Succession broke out, he first served in Italy. In 1702, he was given his first independent command on the upper Rhine.

According to his contemporaries, Villars was, 'boastful to the point of bragging, audacious to make his services valuable and to bring everything to himself, ambitious to rise solidly into the first rank and establish his house and his renown, he missed no opportunity to distinguish himself'. No doubt much of this negative view was down to the fact that he came from the lesser nobility and had risen higher than many nobles of superior standing. On the other hand, he was very popular with his troops, paying much greater attention to their needs than most French generals of the time.

He gained his marshal's baton for his 'victory' at the Battle of Friedlingen (1702). Living up to his boastful reputation, he penned a report of victory to Louis XIV before the battle was over, and before the French were forced to withdraw with many more casualties than the defending Imperialists. His reputation as a successful general was, however, secured. Friedlingen has gone down in the history books as a French victory thanks to Villars' foresight in sending off the first dispatch.

This tendency to seize the initiative was characteristic. Driven by the desire to raise his station, Villars was prepared to take calculated risks and offensive action. In this respect, he had more in common with Marlborough and Eugene than other French generals of the time. Most of the latter were more interested in preserving their status, which made them risk-averse.

In 1703, Villars succeeded in breaking through the Imperialist defences at Kehl on the upper Rhine. He then led his army through the Black Forest to link up with the Bavarians and defeat the Imperialists at the Battle of Höchstädt. He resigned his command when the Bavarians refused to follow through with his plan to advance on Vienna.

Villars was a very ambitious man. Friedlingen had made him a marshal of France, but prestige and standing in Louis XIV's kingdom came from titles of nobility. As a mere marquis, Villars ranked below barons, counts and dukes. In 1705, after two years of intensive lobbying, the king granted him the title of Duc de Villars – raising him to the highest rank available to a noble without royal blood.

From 1704 to 1708, Villars had a number of minor commands, suppressing a French Protestant rebellion and campaigning along the Rhine and Mosel. In 1706, he turned down an offer of command in Italy under the Duc d'Orléans (son of Louis XIV's brother). In his letter to Versailles, Villars wrote that he was not well suited to simultaneously managing a prince and his court as well as an army. He was holding out for another independent command.

In the desperate circumstances of early 1709, Louis XIV turned to Villars to take command of the demoralized army of northern France against an impending attack by the Allies. Villars' predecessors – Tallard, Villeroi, Vendôme and Burgundy – had all met catastrophic defeat when they faced Marlborough in battle. Villars was Louis' last hope.

Claude Louis Hector, Duc de Villars, commanded the French army at Malplaquet. He was loved by his men, but not by his peers. Malplaquet secured his reputation as France's most successful marshal of the War of the Spanish Succession. (Christophel Fine Art/Universal Images Group via Getty Images)

Villars' arrival at Cambrai on 18 March 1709 was greeted enthusiastically by the French soldiers. Lacking food, pay and clothing, their situation was dire to the point of desperation. Villars did what he could to relieve their suffering by requisitioning food and arm-twisting local notables to contribute to the war effort. Supplies began to trickle in, even though the countryside was facing famine. Many new recruits joined the army as a way of avoiding starvation.

By the end of June, Villars had managed to raise his army to the point that it might actually be able to fight. 'The intendants [quartermasters] and the main officers appeared aghast and dejected but Villars did not … One had an extreme confidence in the Maréchal de Villars' (Lefebvre d'Orval, June 1709).

Although technically an Allied victory, Malplaquet saved France, and Villars was seen by many as the saviour. After Britain betrayed the Alliance, Villars defeated Eugene at Denain in 1712. Although a relatively minor battle, his victory cemented Villars' reputation as France's most successful general of the war. Even today, fresh flowers are often laid at the Malplaquet battlefield monuments commemorating Villars.

Louis-François, Duc de Boufflers (1644–1711)

Born into an ancient noble family, Boufflers was 65 years old when he commanded the French right wing at Malplaquet.

Commissioned into the Gardes Françaises in 1662 and rising to command the regiment, Boufflers distinguished himself in the Franco-Dutch and the Nine Years' wars. He became a marshal of France in 1693.

When the War of the Spanish Succession broke out, Boufflers was the highest-ranking marshal of France, and was given command of the army in Flanders. He was relieved of command in 1703 after an unsuccessful campaign that saw many towns fall to the Allies. It looked like his military career was over, but Boufflers' successors fared far worse than he had, suffering disastrous defeats at Blenheim, Ramillies, Turin and Oudenarde.

When the Allies prepared to besiege Lille in 1708, Boufflers petitioned the king to command the garrison. This was granted. Although the city eventually fell, Boufflers' determined defence re-established his reputation.

In the winter of 1708/09, Boufflers was given command of the French army in Flanders with the hope of retaking Lille. The sorry state of the army and complete lack of supplies made it abundantly clear that this was not going to happen. It took all Boufflers' energy to attempt to bring the army up to a state where it could at least defend itself.

Madame de Maintenon, one of the king's mistresses, had this to say of his efforts: 'The Maréchal de Boufflers works as much by himself as all of our ministers together. He tries to untangle the horrible mess into which our generals have let the army fall.'

In the end it was too much for him. Plagued by illness, he asked the king to be recalled. In March 1709, he was replaced by Villars, his former subordinate. When the Allied attack threatened in early September, Boufflers asked permission to rejoin the army as a 'volunteer'. Despite his seniority, he turned down an offer of command from Villars. His letter of reply said: 'Be sure that it is with the greatest joy that I could have and this will always be to receive your orders. You are more worthy, by all reason, to give them.'

In an age and a kingdom where rank and social status was everything, Boufflers' offer to place himself under Villars' command was an act of rare generosity – subordinating pride and personal prestige to the common good. Although he had little experience in open battle, Boufflers acquitted himself well at Malplaquet. He died of natural causes two years later, his reputation fully restored.

Louis-François, Duc de Boufflers, was the most senior marshal of France. He was 65 years old in 1709, and asked the king if he could rejoin the army as a volunteer to serve under Villars, even though he was senior to him. (API/Gamma-Rapho via Getty Images)

Pierre de Montesquiou, Comte d'Artagnan (1640–1725)

D'Artagnan commanded the far right flank of the French army at Malplaquet. The fictional d'Artagnan of Alexandre Dumas' *The Three Musketeers* is largely based on de Montesquiou's uncle.

Like his fictional namesake, d'Artagnan rose through the ranks of the Gardes Françaises, reaching the rank of lieutenant-general by the end of the Nine Years' War. In 1706, he commanded the desperate defence of Ramillies in the battle of the same name. While not quite living up to Dumas' tales of derring-do, he had proven that he could conduct a stubborn defence against the odds. He did the same at Malplaquet, this time with the odds in his favour.

French records from July 1709 list half the army of Flanders under d'Artagnan's command before Boufflers' arrival. D'Artagnan served gallantly under Boufflers during the battle, in which he was wounded and had three horses shot from under him. King Louis XIV appointed d'Artagnan a marshal of France two days after Malplaquet.

Armand de Mormès, Seigneur de Saint-Hilaire (1652–1740)

Lieutenant-General Saint-Hilaire commanded the French artillery at Malplaquet.

At a time when artillery was seen as a subsidiary arm, Saint-Hilaire was an active exponent of more innovative tactics that would fully integrate artillery with the other combat arms. Before the War of the Spanish Succession, he collaborated with the famous engineer Sébastien Le Prestre de Vauban to write a proposal to reform and professionalize the French artillery.

A French marshal's coat from the War of the Spanish Succession. Villars and Boufflers would have worn coats similar to this. (National Army Museum, London)

'The proper use of artillery and bombs [mortars and howitzers] requires an exact art with precise rules that not a single one of these people know … This does not surprise me, because they are only infantrymen that serve the cannon and who obey the artillery officers only when it pleases them … It is often the case that more than half or two-thirds of the rounds are squandered or miss the target completely.'

At Malplaquet, Saint-Hilaire had the opportunity to show the potential of well-sighted guns deployed in massed batteries at critical points. A 20-gun battery, hidden in an enfilade position, tore apart the Dutch attack.

In the early 18th century, when an army withdrew from the field, most of its guns would inevitably be captured. This was due to the fact that the civilian limber teams would be hard to find when the soldiers were in retreat. Saint-Hilaire was able to save 66 of his 80 guns – quite a remarkable feat for the time.

François, Comte d'Albergotti (1654–1717)

Hailing from Florence, d'Albergotti served in the French Royal-Italien regiment during the Franco-Dutch War, eventually becoming colonel of the regiment. Still serving in the French army at the outbreak of the War of the Spanish Succession, he first saw service in Italy, and was promoted to lieutenant-general in 1702. Transferred to Flanders in 1707, he saw action at Oudenarde.

At Malplaquet, he commanded the 21 French battalions that defended the Bois de Sars against an attack by more than 80 Allied battalions. Wounded in the desperate struggle, he survived to command French troops until the end of the war. In his memoirs, Villars wrote that d'Albergotti 'was very brave, and whom I esteemed'.

THE ALLIES

John Churchill, Duke of Marlborough, was Britain's most successful general of all time. The portrait is after Godfrey Kneller. (Universal History Archive/Universal Images Group via Getty Images)

John Churchill, Duke of Marlborough (1650–1722)

Marlborough must surely be counted as Britain's finest military commander of all time. His decisive victories at Blenheim, Ramillies and Oudenarde were tactical masterpieces comparable with those of history's greatest generals. Malplaquet was the closest he ever came to being defeated. He was not only a great tactician, but also had a clear strategic vision, even though this was often undermined by political wrangling in the Allied capitals.

The fractious Alliance was largely kept together thanks to Marlborough's political nous and diplomatic manoeuvrings. In this, he was greatly helped by his wife Sarah, who held enormous influence at Queen Anne's English court.

Marlborough's military career began in 1667 as a 17-year-old ensign in King Charles II's Foot Guards. During the Franco-Dutch War, he led English troops serving in the French army, and was given the rank of colonel by Louis XIV. After the war, he rose through the ranks of the English army, and was largely responsible for James II's victory over Protestant rebels at the Battle of Sedgemoor (1685). He deserted James for William of Orange in the Glorious Revolution of 1688. Although he distinguished himself in a number of actions

ZEGENPRAAL *der* BONDGENÖTEN *by* BERGEN | VICTOIRE, *REMPORTÉE par ses* ALLIES, *sur les* FRANÇOIS
Op. de FRANSEN *bevocht. 11 sept.* 1709 *Uitgegeeft door* A. ALLARD *Amst.* | *Pres de* MONS *Le 11 Sept.* 1709 *Mis en Lumiere, par* A. ALLARD *à Amst.*

A Dutch print commemorating the Allied victory at Malplaquet, emphasising the heroism of the Dutch forces. The middle ground shows blocks of pikemen, but by 1709, pikes were no longer used. (Rijksmuseum Amsterdam; public domain)

during the Nine Years' War, Marlborough was suspected of maintaining Jacobite sympathies, and was never fully trusted by William and Mary. This was exacerbated by jealousies between Queen Mary and her younger sister Anne (heir to the English throne), whom Sarah Churchill served as lady-in-waiting and friend.

Queen Mary's death in 1694 brought about a reconciliation between King William and Princess Anne. It also brought the Marlboroughs back into favour. When the War of the Spanish Succession broke out, King William made Marlborough ambassador to the United Dutch Provinces with the command of English troops sent to the Netherlands.

With the death of King William early in 1702, Anne became queen and Marlborough was raised to the rank of duke (he had been the Earl of Marlborough). The Dutch agreed to his appointment as Captain-General of the army of the Maritime Powers. This post, created by and for William of Orange, was not quite supreme commander of the combined Dutch–English army. It might have been so when the Dutchman William of Orange was also King of England, but the Dutch States General (legislature) refused to give Marlborough a free hand with Dutch troops. Although Dutch generals were technically under Marlborough's command, he had to act in concert with deputies appointed by the States General to ensure Dutch political interests were maintained.

In an age when armies tended to manoeuvre for position and withdraw if the situation was unfavourable, Marlborough was an uncharacteristically aggressive commander. He actively sought out the enemy, and made plans to destroy him in open battle. This rarely went down well with the Dutch

Marlborough owed much of his success to his wife Sarah, who was Queen Anne's favourite lady-in-waiting. She managed the politics on the home front while he fought abroad. (Charles Phelps Cushing/ ClassicStock/Getty Images)

A painting of Marlborough and Eugene meeting after their victory at Blenheim. These two great generals saw eye to eye, and formed a partnership that delivered another victory at Oudenarde and was renewed at Malplaquet. (Painting by Robert Alexander Hillingford)

deputies, who were loath to risk Dutch lives in any risky enterprise.

In 1704, when he marched the army of the Maritime Powers from Flanders to the Danube, Marlborough had to disguise his intentions, not only from the French but also from his political masters. His decisive victory at Blenheim stopped the French from knocking Austria out of the war. It was duly celebrated in Allied capitals, and Marlborough got Blenheim Palace out of it. His masterstroke did not, however, give the Allied governments a greater taste for bold action. Political failure to follow up the victories of 1704 squandered the success, and gave Louis XIV time to rest and recoup. An almost identical situation occurred after Marlborough's victory at Ramillies in 1706.

It was somewhat different after Marlborough's victory at Oudenarde and the capture of Lille in 1708. Now over-confident, the Allied powers rejected Louis' offer of peace, and were poised to invade France. Although political opposition to the war was growing in Britain (England and Scotland having become one country in 1707), the Dutch were keen to win further concessions from France. They were, therefore, less reticent about taking offensive action than they had been in previous years. Furthermore, Austria had reinforced Marlborough with an Imperial army under Prince Eugene.

That Malplaquet was not the victory the Allied powers had hoped for was the beginning of the end for Marlborough. Anti-war sentiment swept the opposition Tories into power in Britain. Lady Masham replaced Sarah Churchill as Queen Anne's favourite, and Sarah was dismissed from court. Marlborough was recalled from his command, and Britain opened secret negotiations for a separate peace with France.

His disgraceful treatment by an ungrateful country was a sad end to the career of Britain's most brilliant general. His success in war was unparalleled due largely to his ability to see a way to victory even when it defied conventional wisdom. This was combined with personal courage, a gift for logistical planning and the ability to manage a fractious alliance. It is true that he took risks, but he only did so after meticulous planning and preparation. Always concerned about the welfare of his soldiers, he did his best to make sure that they had what they needed.

Prince Eugene of Savoy was born in the French court of Versailles, but King Louis XIV turned down his request for a commission in the French army. He switched his allegiance to the Holy Roman Emperor, and became the most successful imperial general of the age. This portrait was painted by Jacob Van Schuppen in 1718. (Sepia Times/Universal Images Group via Getty Images)

He pushed them hard, but he had their trust and they were confident that 'Corporal John' would always lead them to victory.

Much of the credit for Marlborough's success as Captain-General of the Maritime Powers needs to go to his wife Sarah. It was her influence that secured his appointment in the first place. She was able to manage the politics in England, leaving him to concentrate on the politics and fighting abroad. Once she fell from grace, so did he. His removal from command in 1711 was in part due to English war-weariness, exacerbated by the huge losses at Malplaquet, and partly because Sarah had lost her influence at court.

Prince François Eugene of Savoy (1663–1736)

Born in Paris and growing up at the court of Versailles, Eugene was the best French commander Louis XIV never had. Eugene's mother was caught up in the many intrigues at Versailles, including the endemic poisonings in the 1670s as courtiers sought to do away with their rivals. For this reason, Eugene's application for a commission in the French army was turned down by Louis.

Intent on a military career, Eugene moved to Vienna, where his offer of service was accepted by the emperor. He first saw action at the age of 20, helping to defend Vienna against the siege by the Ottoman Turks in 1683. He won fame as a first-rate commander when he decisively defeated the Turks at the Battle of Zenta in 1697.

Eugene was sent to command the Imperial army in Italy when the War of the Spanish Succession broke out, defeating the French at the battles of Carpi and Chiari. Louis XIV wrote a letter to his generals in which he said of Eugene: 'I have warned you that you are dealing with an enterprising young prince. He does not tie himself down to the rules of war.' Perhaps Louis was already regretting his decision to refuse Eugene's earlier request for a commission in the French army.

A man who did not 'tie himself down to the rules of war' was Marlborough's kindred spirit. Their partnership at Blenheim produced one of the greatest Allied victories of the war. This partnership continued throughout the conflict, with Eugene and Marlborough seeing eye to eye what needed to be done, even when their respective political masters thought otherwise. While the combined efforts of Eugene and Marlborough formed a partnership made in heaven, Eugene had further successes on his own – most notably his victory at Turin, which effectively ended the war in Italy.

Malplaquet again brought Eugene and Marlborough together, with Eugene commanding the Allied right wing. After Marlborough's dismissal, Eugene took his place as captain-general, but with the British desertion of the Alliance, he was defeated by Villars at Denain in 1712. He helped to negotiate favourable peace terms between France and the Holy Roman Empire in 1714.

After the War of the Spanish Succession, Eugene led the Imperial army against the Turks, winning a decisive victory at the Battle of Belgrade (1716). He continued to lead the Imperial army in numerous engagements until the end of the War of the Polish Succession in 1735.

Johann Matthias, Reichsgraf von der Schulenburg (1661–1747)

Originally from Saxony, Schulenburg saw action in the Imperial army against the Turks in the 1680s. When the Great Northern War broke out in 1701, he was in the service of Saxony, rising to command the Saxon army. His defeat by the Swedes at Fraustadt in 1706 knocked Saxony out of the war, and Schulenburg again took service in the Imperial army. At Malplaquet, he commanded the 40 battalions under Eugene that formed the main Allied attack on the right wing through the dense woods of the Bois de

ABOVE LEFT
Johann Matthias, Reichsgraf von der Schulenburg, from Saxony commanded 40 battalions on the Allied right wing at Malplaquet. (The Picture Art Collection/Alamy)

ABOVE RIGHT
Claude-Frédéric t'Serclaes, Graaf van Tilly was in overall command of the Dutch at Malplaquet. He took no active part in the battle. (Icom Images/Alamy)

Sars. In 1711, he was recruited by Venice to defend their far-flung possessions against the Ottoman Turks.

Carl Philipp, Reichsgraf von Wylich und Lottum (1650–1719)

Lottum was appointed to command the Prussian troops in the service of the Maritime Powers when the War of the Spanish Succession broke out. He fought at Blenheim and played a significant role at Oudenarde, holding the thin Allied centre against a French counter-attack. At Malplaquet, he commanded 22 battalions that fought their way into the Bois de Sars to support Schulenburg's attack. He was promoted to field marshal of the Prussian army in 1713.

Claude Frédéric t'Serclaes, Graaf van Tilly (1648–1723)

Tilly was promoted to the rank of field marshal on the death of Hendrik van Nassau-Ouwerkerk in 1708. This made him the most senior Dutch officer at Malplaquet. He had a long military career reaching back to 1667, when he entered Spanish service, later fighting for the Dutch as a cavalry officer in the Franco-Dutch War and Nine Years' War.

Tilly commanded the English and Dutch cavalry on the Allied right at Ramillies, and the Dutch and Danish cavalry at Oudenarde. In overall command of the Dutch at Malplaquet, Tilly took almost no part in the Dutch attack that was led by the Prince of Orange.

Only 22 years old, Johan Willem Friso van Oranje-Nassau – the Prince of Orange – commanded the Dutch attack at Malplaquet. This portrait by Lancelot Volders was painted in 1710. (The Picture Art Collection/Alamy)

Johan Willem Friso van Oranje-Nassau, Prince of Orange (1687–1711)

Nephew of King William III, the Prince of Orange was technically heir to William's Dutch titles and possessions, although he never fully realized them. His claim to the Principality of Orange was disputed by the Prussians, who had a counter-claim. This tiny principality around the city of Orange in Provence was eventually ceded to France at the end of the War of the Spanish Succession.

The young prince commanded a contingent of Dutch cavalry under Tilly at Oudenarde in 1708, and took part in the siege of Lille later that year. Only 22 years old at Malplaquet, he led the Dutch attack on French entrenchments, with courage bordering on recklessness. Whether or not he exceeded his orders, leading to horrendous Dutch casualties, is still debated by historians.

He died in a drowning accident two years after Malplaquet.

OPPOSING FORCES

THE FRENCH ARMY

Louis XIV built the French army up from an ill-disciplined collection of semi-independent units into a professional, national, fighting force. By the end of the 17th century, it was the best-trained, best-led and most professionally organized army in Europe. It was also huge, rising from 150,000 men in 1679 to nearly half a million at the height of the War of the Spanish Succession. In comparison, the Holy Roman Empire – France's most powerful rival – only fielded 100,000 men in 1705, and the British army was 75,000-strong in 1710.

Maintaining such numbers of men took its toll on the French populace, as the king could not rely on volunteers alone. In every town and village, additional young men were chosen for the army by lottery. Those drawing a black slip of paper were conscripted. In many places, families held a funeral service in advance, anticipating that their son would end up buried somewhere far from home.

Bivouac – a painting of French troops resting at the end of a march at the time of Malplaquet, by Jean-Antoine Watteau. (Fine Art Images/ Heritage Images/Getty Image)

The French army at the outbreak of the War of the Spanish Succession benefitted from regular pay, a good commissariat and a clear line of command under Louis' autocratic rule. It was hampered by its previous success. Confident in their supremacy, the French were slow to take up new tactical innovations. The illusion of supremacy was broken at Blenheim in 1704. By 1709, the French army had suffered defeat after defeat and was a shadow of its former self.

With the economy in ruins, famine stalked the countryside and the soldiers went without pay, clothing, ammunition and food. In the winter of 1708/09, many men died of starvation. In a letter of 17 June, Marshal Villars wrote: 'Only a single day of bread was delivered today and that arrived only in the evening, such that the soldiers worked all day without eating.'

This contemporary print by Jean-Antoine Watteau shows French recruits on their way to join the army. Many new recruits joined Villars' army as a way of avoiding starvation. (The Metropolitan Museum of Art; public domain)

The cavalry

At the end of the 17th century, the reputation of the French cavalry was so high that opponents would take precautions to find terrain or circumstances that would inhibit their ability to manoeuvre. Their reputation was shattered at Blenheim, when the elite French Gendarmes were defeated by a smaller number of English horse. There was a similar outcome at Ramillies in 1706. The French horse favoured advancing to within a few paces of their opponents, discharging pistols and then charging with swords. The English and Dutch had begun to adopt Swedish tactics, charging into combat with swords alone without pausing to fire their pistols. This gave them an edge if the charge was pressed home with confidence.

A contemporary engraving of cavalry combat. Two troopers are engaged in a close life and death struggle, while the background shows horsemen using their pistols. (Pubic domain)

From Blenheim to Malplaquet, the performance of the French cavalry left much to be desired. Possibly too much has been made of the supremacy of the English and Dutch cavalry tactics. Giving fire as well as closing with swords did have some benefits, and good French cavalry officers evolved their tactics as the war progressed. Their successful actions at Malplaquet did much to restore their tarnished reputation.

Maison du Roi (King's Household)

These were the elite of the French army, with the very best men, horses and equipment. The Maison du Roi included four companies of the

This sketch by Jean-Antoine Watteau shows drummers of the French army at the time of Malplaquet. It gives a realistic impression of the dress and demeanour of the ordinary soldiers of the time, in contrast to most illustrations, which depict a more romanticized impression. (Art Collection 2/Alamy)

Gardes du Corps (Body Guards); one company of Gendarmes de la Garde (Men-at-Arms of the Guard); one company of Chevaux-légers de la Garde (Light Horse of the Guard); two companies of Mousquetaires du Roi (King's Musketeers); and one company of Grenadiers à Cheval (Horse Grenadiers). Each company comprised 200 men. The Maison du Roi fought as a single brigade, usually held in reserve. At Malplaquet, they were positioned behind the centre at the critical juncture between Villars' and Boufflers' wings.

Gendarmes (Men-at-Arms)

Descended from the knights and men-at-arms of previous centuries, the Gendarmes were second in seniority to the Maison du Roi. Distinguished by their red uniform, the Gendarmes were very well equipped and had high status. There were 16 companies at Malplaquet, which varied in strength from 80 to 200 men per company. Like the Maison du Roi, they formed a single brigade and were also deployed in the centre.

Chevaux-légers (Light Horse)

These were the line cavalry of the French army. The name is misleading to modern readers, as they were not light cavalry as we now understand the term. The light designation is a throwback to earlier times, when the Gendarmes were fully armoured and others were not. Body armour had been abandoned long before Malplaquet, and the only distinction was status, which ensured that the Gendarmes had a priority for recruits, horses, pay and equipment. Most *chevaux-légers* wore grey–white coats, usually with red cuffs, although royal regiments and some others had blue. Regiments varied in strength from two to three squadrons, averaging about 150 men each. The squadron, not the regiment, was the basic fighting unit. Squadrons of the same regiment could be deployed in different places on the battlefield, just as the battalions of a multi-battalion infantry regiment might be.

Carabiniers

Deriving their name from the carbines they carried, these men previously formed an elite company in each regiment of *chevaux-légers*. By the time of the War of the Spanish Succession they were brigaded together to form a single unit of ten squadrons, each of 80 men. At Malplaquet, they formed a reserve brigade on the left flank. They were distinguished from the *chevaux-légers* by their blue coats with red cuffs.

Dragoons

These were mounted infantry who used horses for mobility, but would usually dismount to fight as skirmishers on foot. The nags they rode were smaller and weaker than true cavalry horses, and they were not well trained for mounted combat. The men had lower status than the *chevaux-légers* and were paid less. They were most useful for scouting, screening, foraging or internal security duties. In contrast to Allied practice, the French never deployed their dragoons in line of battle alongside the *chevaux-légers*. A brigade of dragoons occupied a reserve position on the left flank at Malplaquet, and those that fought, did so on foot.

The infantry

Most French infantry regiments had several battalions, with each battalion comprising around 600 men at full strength. The older regiments usually had two or three battalions, while those more recently raised tended to have only one battalion. A few, such as the Regiment du Roi and Regiment d'Alsace, had four battalions each.

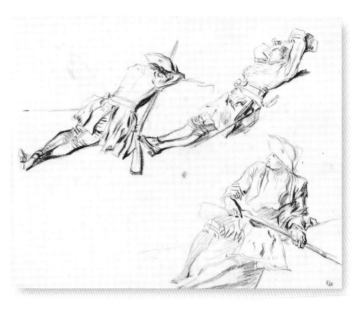

This contemporary sketch shows French soldiers snatching a few moments of rest as they wait in their positions for a potential attack. This is how most men in both armies would have spent the night of 10 September 1709. (Jean-Antoine Watteau)

Usually formed five ranks deep, the French fired by ranks – the front rank firing first, then passing to the rear to reload as the second rank gave fire, and so on. This was the way musketeers had operated for the better part of a century. It allowed the battalion to maintain a constant rate of fire, delivered by each one of the five ranks in succession.

At Malplaquet, the average strength of a French battalion was only 300–400 men. It is quite possible that they deployed three ranks deep rather than the usual five, keeping more or less the same frontage as a full-strength battalion. The infantry of the Maritime Powers deployed three ranks deep, and by the end of the war this had become the norm.

Gardes Françaises and Suisses

Part of the Maison du Roi, these were the elite foot of the French army, each forming a brigade of several thousand men. Wearing blue coats, the Gardes Françaises were recruited from Frenchmen, while the red-coated Gardes Suisses were Swiss. Four battalions of the former were present at Malplaquet, and two battalions of the latter. They were deployed together in the entrenchments on the left flank of Boufflers' wing. Their performance in the battle did not live up to their elite status.

French Line

The majority of the French foot wore grey–white coats, usually with red or blue cuffs. The most senior regiments – the Vieux Corps – had grey–white cuffs. Of these, Picardie, Piedmont, Navarre and Champagne were present at Malplaquet, each with three battalions.

Foreign troops

The French army included a large number of Irish, German, Swiss, Walloon and Italian battalions. The Irish Brigade occupied the centre redans at Malplaquet, while men from Bavaria and Cologne were to their right. Other German, Swiss, Walloon and Italian troops were dispersed along the line. The

This sketch of French soldiers by Jean-Antoine Watteau was drawn four or five years after Malplaquet. All soldiers of the time had similar uniforms and equipment. (Fondation Custodia, Collection Frits Lugt, Paris)

Spanish army of the Netherlands was under French command at the time. Their foot were garrisoning Mons, but several squadrons of Spanish horse and dragoons fought at Malplaquet.

Grenadiers

Each infantry battalion had a company of grenadiers, formed from the tallest and strongest soldiers. Their name was derived from the hand grenades they carried, but by 1709, these were rarely used in open battle. The Imperialists often brigaded their grenadiers together to form elite composite battalions. The French usually kept the grenadier companies with their parent units, but at Malplaquet a number were drawn from their battalions to form a composite battalion of grenadiers, which held the far-right flank.

Artillery

Artillery at this time was very much a subsidiary arm. Driven into place by civilian limber teams, the guns were usually spaced out in front of the army to conduct an opening bombardment. Once the lines closed, they rarely had any further impact on the battle. Light guns could be manhandled by infantrymen, but there was no chance that the civilians would come up to the front to move the heavier guns.

The Seigneur de Saint-Hilaire, commanding the French artillery, did not deploy his guns in the traditional manner. Instead of spreading them out equally across the front, or attaching the guns to infantry brigades, he set up several massed batteries of 10–20 guns at key points calculated to inflict the most damage on the enemy.

THE ALLIED ARMIES

The Allied force at Malplaquet comprised two armies that had combined for the 1709 campaign season: the army of the Maritime Powers (Dutch and British) commanded by Marlborough, and the Imperialists under Eugene. Both of these armies comprised men of many different nations. Politically, the Alliance was fractious, but despite their different nationalities, the men had been honed by years of fighting together and a succession of victories. Morale was high, thanks to the success of the 1708 campaign. Units were well supplied and reasonably up to strength.

British

Under Marlborough's leadership the English army – British after the Acts of Union in 1707 – had evolved into an excellent fighting force. French generals were told to look where the British were deployed and expect the main attack

This painting shows Allied troopers (foreground) using carbines and pistols against French horse with drawn swords. At this time, cavalrymen used a combination of firearms and swords in close combat. Marlborough encouraged his horse to charge without pausing to give fire, but the Imperialists tended to rely on firepower. (Public domain)

to be there. This was not the case at Malplaquet, where the majority of British foot were deployed in a thin line under George Douglas-Hamilton, Earl of Orkney to hold the centre, while the main attacks went in on the flanks. All British troops at this time (including artillery) wore red coats with various coloured cuffs.

British regiments of foot were mostly one battalion strong, usually named after their colonel. With over 700 men at full strength, they were larger than French battalions. Deploying three ranks deep, they had a much wider frontage than the five-rank French formation. Firing by platoons rather than by ranks, a British battalion could deliver continuous firepower over the same frontage as two French battalions.

The 19 British battalions at Malplaquet

1st Guards	(Grenadier)
2nd Guards	(Coldstream)
Orkney	(Royal Scots)
Argyll	(3rd Foot, The Buffs)
Webb	(8th Foot, King's)
North and Grey	(10th Foot, later the Royal Anglians)
Howe	(15th Foot, later the Prince of Wales' Yorkshire Regiment)
Godfrey	(16th Foot)
Ingoldsby	(18th Foot, the Royal Irish)
Erle	(19th Foot, later the Green Howards)
de Lalo	(21st Foot, later the Royal Scots Fusiliers)
Sabine	(23rd Foot, later the Royal Welch Fusiliers)
Primrose	(24th Foot, later the Royal Regiment of Wales)
Preston	(26th Foot, The Cameronians)
Meredith	(37th Foot, later the Royal Hampshires)
Orrery	(disbanded after the war)
Temple	(disbanded after the war)
Evans	(disbanded after the war)
Pendergast	(disbanded after the war)

Most of these battalions held the centre under the command of the Earl of Orkney. Some came up late from Tournai with Lieutenant-General Henry Withers, while others were part of Count Lottum's force.

At Blenheim, a smaller number of British horse defeated the elite French Gendarmes, destroying the reputation of French cavalry superiority. Marlborough favoured a mounted charge in a relatively thin formation only two ranks deep, with a second line following up behind. Unlike the French, who often paused to fire pistols, the British tended to close with cold steel only. This gave greater impetus to the charge, but risked casualties from enemy pistol and carbine fire as they closed to contact.

The British cavalry contingent at Malplaquet consisted of nine squadrons of horse and six squadrons of dragoons. They were deployed as a single brigade under Lieutenant-General Wood as a second line in the centre of the battlefield. British dragoons at this time fought as cavalry, rather than mounted infantry. Paid less than horse and riding inferior mounts, they were not quite of the same calibre as true horse, but on many occasions they fared well in mounted combat with French horse. The North British Dragoons (later the Royal Scots Greys) particularly distinguished themselves at Malplaquet. After the war, the British government redesignated all mounted troops as 'dragoons'. This was purely a cost-saving measure, as dragoons were paid less than horse.

Dutch

Under Marlborough's command, the Dutch used the same tactics and formations as the British. Their foot gave fire by platoons, their horse charged with cold steel rather than firing pistols and their dragoons fought as cavalry.

Dutch forces were raised in each of the United Provinces. These were Holland, Zeeland, Utrecht, Friesland, Groningen, Overijssel and Guelderland. Most Dutch troops wore grey–white coats with variously coloured cuffs. Many dragoons wore red coats, while the elite Gardes te Voet (Foot Guards) and Gardes te Paard (Horse Guards) had blue coats. Most foot regiments had only one battalion, but the Gardes te Voet had three, and the Prince of Orange's regiment had two.

The Dutch foot formed the left wing of the Allied army at Malplaquet. Thirty battalions strong, they attacked the French entrenchments, suffering enormous casualties.

The native troops were supplemented by a number of foreign regiments. Amongst the 30 battalions at Malplaquet were the following:

Nationality	Commander(s)
one battalion of Swedes	Oxenstiern
one battalion of Walloons	Fournier
two battalions of Scots	Tullibardine and Hepburn
nine battalions of Swiss	Dohna-Ferrassieré, Schmid de Grüneck (2), Gabriel May (2), Stürler (2) and Mestral (2)

The Gardes te Voet initially had two battalions on the left flank, but they were later joined by a third battalion which came up late from Tournai. Two additional battalions of Walloons from the Dutch army – Caris (or Carl Rex) and Delsupeché – were deployed with the Imperialists, and later became part of the Imperial army.

The Dutch cavalry at Malplaquet formed the largest contingent of Marlborough's mounted reserve in the centre of the battlefield. Commanded by the Prince d'Auvergne, this force comprised 62 squadrons, of which

13 were dragoons. Included amongst the horse were four squadrons of guards. Another 21 squadrons were deployed to support the Dutch foot on the left.

Prussians

Prussia was technically part of the Holy Roman Empire, but managed to gain the status of an independent kingdom in exchange for the large numbers of troops it provided for the Maritime Powers. They were paid for by the British and Dutch, and served under Marlborough's command. The contract of 12 April 1709 had 19 battalions in the pay of the Maritime Powers. At Malplaquet, one battalion (Mecklenberg-Schwerin) was assigned to command the baggage. Another battalion that should have been present (Varenne) is not mentioned in any contemporary records of the battle, so they may have been either in the siege lines at Mons or elsewhere on garrison duties. Friedrich Wilhelm von Grumbkow's battalion was captured in 1708 and is also not mentioned, although Grumbkow himself was present at the battle.

Reichsgraf von Wylich und Lottum commanded 22 battalions that attacked the Bois de Sars, of which at least 14 were Prussians. Reichsgraf Finck von Finckenstein commanded several battalions between Orkney's British and Major-General Jorgen Rantzau's Hanoverians at Malplaquet. Most of the Prussian battalions can be accounted for in Lottum's command, therefore it is highly likely that Finck's command included some British battalions that Imperial archives of June 1709 record as being brigaded with Prussians.

Wearing dark blue coats, usually with red cuffs, the Prussian foot were not yet the fearsome infantry of later years, but they distinguished themselves at Malplaquet. Their battalions were relatively small – around 600 men at full strength. They probably fought in the same way as their Dutch and British paymasters – firing by platoons in a three-rank formation.

According to the contracts of 1709, Prussia also provided 23 squadrons of horse and 16 of dragoons. Most of these fought at Malplaquet, brigaded with the Hanoverians in the centre under the command of the Hanoverian Josua von Bülow.

The reputation of the Prussian cavalry was not as high as that of their foot. It may be that they still preferred traditional tactics, pausing to give fire with pistols before charging home. Like the Dutch and British, the Prussian dragoons fought as second-rate cavalry rather than mounted infantry. Most horse and dragoons wore white–grey coats.

This grenadier cap is from the time of Malplaquet and belonged to a soldier of Ingoldsby's regiment (Royal Irish). Captain Parker of the Royal Irish left an account of his regiment's action at Malplaquet. It was in the possession of his family for generations, but could not have been his, as it is not an officer's cap. (National Army Museum, London)

In the notoriously wet weather of Flanders, soldiers wore capes to help keep themselves dry and warm. They would not have been worn in battle. (Jean-Antoine Watteau)

Danes

Although fighting a war with Sweden at the time, Denmark hired out a large number of troops to both the Imperialists and the Maritime Powers. In 1709, those Danes contracted to the Imperialists were serving in Hungary and Italy. Nine battalions of foot, 16 squadrons of horse and five squadrons of dragoons were in the pay of the Maritime Powers in 1709. Most of these fought at Malplaquet. They did not, however, fight under Marlborough's command. Instead, they were assigned to the Imperialists.

Almost all of the Danes – cavalry and infantry – wore white–grey coats. However, the Livgarden til Fot (Foot Guards) wore straw-yellow coats with red cuffs, and the Livregiment til Hest (Horse Guards) wore red coats with yellow cuffs. One battalion of foot guards and two squadrons of horse guards were present at Malplaquet. The Danish cavalry were noted for wearing tough elk-skin coats over their uniforms.

Hanoverians

In their red coats the Hanoverians were almost indistinguishable from the British, and they would soon share a ruler (Prince George of Hanover became King George I of Britain in 1714). Their military organization and tactics were similarly indistinguishable from the British, and some contemporary accounts treat them as almost one and the same.

Hanover supplied 14 infantry battalions, 14 squadrons of horse and 15 of dragoons under contract to the Maritime Powers. Not all of these fought at Malplaquet. Some were left behind to garrison Tournai, others maintained the siege lines at Mons.

Commanded by von Bülow, the Hanoverian cavalry were brigaded together with the Prussians. Four infantry battalions of Hanoverians under Rantzau held the left of the Allied centre; some may also have been with Lottum. An additional 1,900 men – most probably Hanoverians – came up later from Mons.

Hessians

Hesse-Kassel provided ten battalions of foot, ten squadrons of horse and eight squadrons of dragoons under contract to the Maritime Powers. All of these were at Malplaquet. Like the Danes, they actually fought under Eugene's command rather than Marlborough's. Most of the foot joined Schulenburg's attack on the Bois de Sars, others came up with Henry Withers from Tournai. The Prince of Hesse-Kassel commanded 21 squadrons of horse that supported the Dutch attack on the left, but these were probably all Dutch. Most of the Hessian horse formed part of the Imperial cavalry reserve, but several squadrons probably took part in Major-General Miklau's flanking action to the west.

Imperialists

The army of the Holy Roman Empire was built around a core of Austrians supplemented by units provided by the various German principalities of the empire. A large number of troops were supplied by other states under contract.

The army's tactics had evolved to meet the empire's greatest threat – the Ottoman Turks. The Imperialists placed great importance on firepower and maintaining good order to stand up to the more numerous Turks with their preponderance of light mobile cavalry. Imperialist cavalry, therefore, formed large regiments of cuirassiers that would advance slowly so as not to fall into disorder – using pistol fire to defeat their lighter, more mobile opponents. Their infantry would deploy in depth, firing by ranks, often with attached light artillery pieces. Imperial dragoons still sometimes dismounted to fight on foot like the French.

The Imperial army also included a number of hussar regiments. These were light cavalry, originally raised from their Hungarian subjects. Most useful for scouting and skirmishing, they rarely formed part of the main cavalry line, but at Malplaquet several squadrons of Imperial hussars took an active role. Later, all European armies raised regiments of hussars to take over the scouting, foraging and skirmishing role formally done by dragoons.

Malplaquet was the first battle the Imperialists fought in Flanders. Imperial cavalry had joined Marlborough at Blenheim, and the Imperialists had fought the French in Italy. Otherwise, their attention was fixed firmly to the east, looking to the Turks and coming to terms with Swedish success against Saxony in the Great Northern War. At the same time, they were also trying to suppress a rebellion in Hungary.

The polyglot nature of the Imperial army can be seen in its composition at Malplaquet. Under the overall leadership of the Franco-Italian Prince Eugene, Schulenburg (from Saxony) commanded the foot that attacked on the Allied right. Thanks to his memoirs, his command is the best attested of all the contingents at the battle. Formed in three lines, it comprised 40 battalions of many different nationalities (see below table). Many of these troops were in the pay of the Maritime Powers, temporarily placed under Eugene's command for the battle.

Prince Eugene's command at Malplaquet

Austria	four battalions
Hesse-Kassel	seven battalions
Munster	one battalion
Ansbach	two battalions
Wallonia	two battalions
Denmark	five battalions
Saxony	seven battalions
Pfalz (Palatinate)	four battalions
Braunschweig-Wolfenbüttel	two battalions
Würzburg	two battalions
Württemberg	two battalions
Mecklenburg	one battalion
Holstein-Gottorf	one battalion

OPPOSING PLANS

THE FRENCH PLAN

Villars' intent was to prevent an Allied invasion of France. The poor state of the French army and the continuing lack of supplies greatly limited his options. An aggressive commander by nature, Villars would have probably preferred an active defence, taking some offensive action to keep his opponents off balance.

Offensive action requires armies to be fed and equipped on the move. Villars could barely achieve that in a static position. The sorry state of France's ability to properly supply her army is shown in the correspondence of the harassed men responsible for feeding and equipping the army:

> It is necessary to bring grain here [to the army] if one does not wish to expose it to famine, insurrection of the people and contagion ... Last year there was only half a crop. This year there won't be anything ... In this extremity if the King judges that he must take the last morsel of bread from his people to give it to his troops, I can only let him with perfect submission. (Archbishop of Cambrai, April 1709)

The more the campaign season approached, the worse the situation. The magazines did not advance, money became more and more rare, officers who arrived with recruits did not find a sol for food. Those that passed the winter on this frontier had sold everything and pawned everything such that most no longer had horses or servants ... Everyone complained greatly and everyone said they were willing, but that they were not in a state to do anything. (Intendant of Flanders, May 1709)

That they 'were willing but not in a state to do anything' perfectly encapsulates the state of the French army as the peace negotiations broke down and the 1709 campaign began. The supply problems did not end, although, through superhuman efforts, they had begun to be overcome,

Tournai was one of the best-fortified towns in Flanders. Villars hoped that a siege would bog the Allies down for the entire 1709 campaign season. (Musée des Armes et de l'Histoire Militaire, Tournai)

Strategic situation, spring 1709: the three Allied options

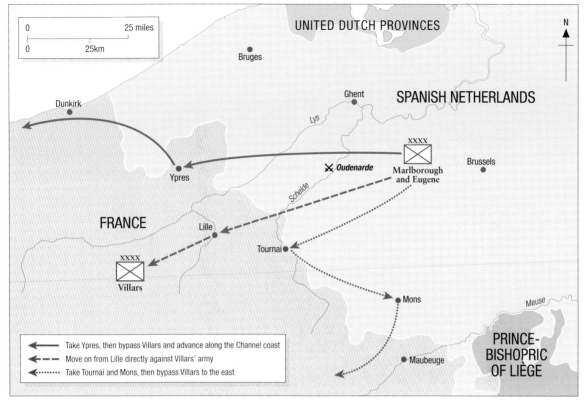

as the Intendant (royal administrator) reports in early August: 'After insurmountable difficulties I have achieved the goal of giving the army enough bread for three days. There is nothing to desire other than this continues.'

Given his supply difficulties, Villars knew that his only hope of preventing an Allied breakthrough was to adopt a strong defensive position that could not easily be bypassed. He also knew that Marlborough and Eugene would not sit idle. Therefore, he had to give them something to do that would buy him enough time to get the French army into better shape.

He entrenched his army in a very strong position about 20km south-west of Allied-occupied Lille. These entrenchments covered a gap between the towns of Douai and Béthune in northern France, blocking the most probable Allied line of advance into France from Lille. They were more than simple protection for an encamped army. French engineers constructed a series of strongpoints with obstructed approaches connected by lines of entrenchments and deep ditches. The position was naturally strengthened by numerous streams and marshes, and became known as the Lines of La Bassée, after the small town where Villars made his headquarters.

Villars calculated that the Allies would not risk attacking such a strong position. If they did, then he would probably be able to see them off. If they did not attack him, what else might they do? In all likelihood, they would turn their attention to one or more of the important French-occupied towns on the flanks – Ypres and Tournai being the prime contenders. If the Allies became bogged down in a siege, then Villars would be able to buy time and prevent an invasion of France. He therefore deliberately refused to reinforce

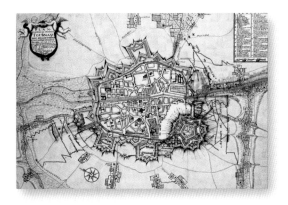

A plan of Tournai at the time of the 1709 siege. (Musée des Armes et de l'Histoire Militaire, Tournai; author's photograph)

the garrisons and withdrew 3,000 troops from Tournai to tempt the Allies to undertake a siege of what was one of the best-fortified towns in Europe.

Tournai was defended by 12 battalions of foot and five squadrons of dragoons – around 6,000 men. They were under the command of the Marquis de Surville-Hautfort, who had distinguished himself at the siege of Lille the previous year. Tournai's defences were in good shape, and Villars calculated that the town should be able to hold out, without reinforcements, until well into the autumn. By then, the campaign season should be too far advanced for the Allies to make any other significant moves. If all went well, Villars might hope that he would have until the following year to rebuild his army in readiness for the inevitable decisive battle. The loss of Tournai would be a small price to pay if it kept the Allies tied up for the entire campaign season.

THE ALLIED PLAN

The Allies wanted to force the French to accept the peace terms they had previously rejected. The varying national interests of the Allied powers made it difficult to come to a clear consensus on the best course of action to make this happen. They had a number of options open to them. They could attack Villars' entrenched army in an attempt to break through; they could try to bypass it by moving along the Channel coast into France; or they could invest and capture key French-held towns, further weakening the French position.

Marlborough may well have preferred to strike along the Channel coast, bypassing Villars' army to the west. This idea did not, however, find any traction with the other Allied commanders, probably because it would leave them exposed to a flank attack.

On 24 June, Marlborough and Eugene advanced on Villars' position to determine if they could successfully attack it directly. William, Earl of Cadogan – Marlborough's quartermaster-general – infiltrated the French lines disguised as a peasant. He reported that the French position was too strong to risk an attack. This left the option of moving on one of the key French-occupied towns. The question remained, which one?

In his memoirs, the Dutch deputy Sicco van Goslinga recounts a council of war that followed:

> Word had been received that Ypres was equipped to present a long and vigorous defence. To the contrary, Tournai had a very weak garrison for a fortress of such importance. The fortress, it is true, is one of the strongest in the universe and that was the reason why de Villars had neglected it, but simple walls do not defend themselves. The Duke of Marlborough voted to besiege Ypres. Prince Eugene voted to besiege Tournai. The others, including the Graaf van Tilly voted with Prince Eugene.

So the Allied plan was to invest Tournai, hoping to take it quickly, and then move on to hopefully force Villars out of his strong position and bring him to battle.

THE OPENING MOVES

Once the Allies had made their decision to invest Tournai, they spread rumours that their intent was to attack Villars' entrenched army. To enhance their deception plan, they withdrew their baggage to Lille, and made a number of demonstrations against the French lines. Villars strengthened his position and made ready to repulse them.

On 26 June, Marlborough and Eugene made a surprise night move towards Tournai. Arriving the following morning, they took the French completely unawares. At 7 a.m., the Prince of Orange with an advance guard of ten battalions and 30 squadrons forced back the French piquets and captured supplies destined for the town. By noon, most of Marlborough's

The campaign, June–September 1709

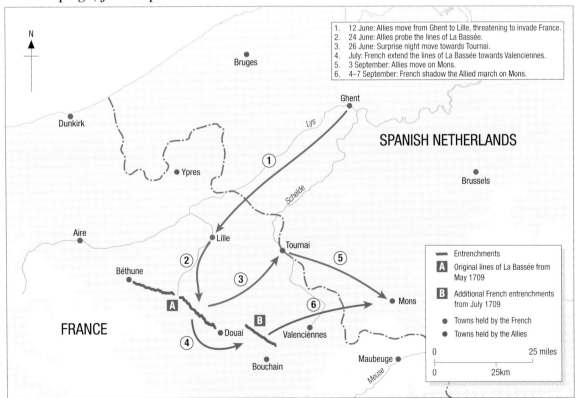

1. 12 June: Allies move from Ghent to Lille, threatening to invade France.
2. 24 June: Allies probe the lines of La Bassée.
3. 26 June: Surprise night move towards Tournai.
4. July: French extend the lines of La Bassée towards Valenciennes.
5. 3 September: Allies move on Mons.
6. 4–7 September: French shadow the Allied march on Mons.

Entrenchments

A Original lines of La Bassée from May 1709

B Additional French entrenchments from July 1709

● Towns held by the French
● Towns held by the Allies

British and Dutch were in position to begin the siege works, with Eugene's Imperialists joining them on the evening of 27 June.

Until this point, both the French and Allied plans for the campaign were unfolding as both had wished. Although Marlborough and Eugene had taken the French unawares by their rapid overnight move on Tournai, Villars' greatest worry was that they might attempt to bypass him to the west:

> It was evident that their objective was, after defeating me, to penetrate as far as Boulogne, and after laying all of Picardy under contribution, to push their detachments as far as Paris … It was a great relief to me that the enemy fixed on a siege of Tournai, which ought to occupy them the whole of the campaign. (Villars' *Memoirs*)

Villars' strategic aim was to keep the Allies bogged down in a protracted siege. Calculating that the Marquis de Surville-Hautfort with 6,000 men could hold out for many months against over 100,000 Allied troops, Villars made no attempt to relieve Tournai. He had not realized that, commanded by the best two generals of their generation, the well-supplied and motivated Allied troops might reduce Tournai in less time than he had calculated. Tournai was to the north-east of Villars' entrenchments. If the Allies took the town in good time, they could then potentially move on the extreme right of the French lines, forcing them to move out to block an advance into France by way of Mons and Valenciennes. Villars, therefore, extended his entrenched lines to the east to cover the gap between Douai and Valenciennes.

THE SIEGE OF TOURNAI

By 6 July, Tournai was fully invested, and the trenches were opened on the evening of the following day. The trenches approached the walls in three places. Schulenburg led an attack from the west, while Lottum and the Dutch Baron François Fagel approached from the east. The heavy artillery, needed for reducing the walls, was delayed by heavy rain, and was not in place until 10 July.

The French conducted an active defence, often sallying out from the town. Villars deliberately did not reinforce the garrison, but he did send out several detachments to harass and disrupt the besiegers. The Allies were also hampered in their attack by numerous mines.

Despite these difficulties, the Allies succeeded in capturing a number of important outer-works on

Painted within a year or two of the Malplaquet campaign, this scene shows French soldiers with their families and camp followers behind the lines. This captures the life of ordinary people in the four months they spent in the Lines of La Bassée. (Painting by Jean-Antoine Watteau)

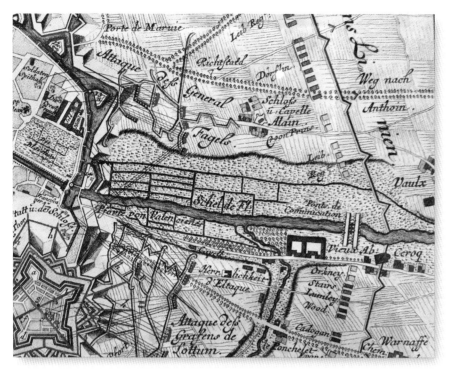

This map shows the attacks conducted by Fagel and Lottum against Tournai's eastern walls in July 1709. The lines in yellow are their siege trenches; the red ones mark the location of their gun batteries. (Musée des Armes et de l'Histoire Militaire, Tournai)

all three of their approaches by 27 July. They then began to prepare for a general assault. The following day, de Surville-Hautfort raised a flag of truce, and on 30 July, he surrendered the town. The terms agreed on allowed the garrison (now reduced to 4,000 men) to retire to the fortified citadel, while the town was handed over to the Allies.

In a letter to his wife Sarah, Marlborough wrote:

> We have at last signed the capitulation of Tournai, so that tomorrow night we shall continue the attack on the citadel. The taking of it, we fear, will cost us more time and men than this of the town. But what gives me the greatest prospect of the happiness of being with you is that certainty the misery of France increases which must bring us peace. The misery of all the poor people we see is such that one must be a brute not to pity them.

As Marlborough had predicted, the well-fortified citadel was a harder nut to crack than the town. Throughout August, fierce fighting took place above and below ground. Casualties were high on both sides, often in horrible conditions. On 15 August, a French sally drove back 150 Allied soldiers, and when they thought they had reached safety, the French ignited a mine that blew them up. This was just one of many such incidents as men tunnelled underground, fighting in darkness, ever fearful of a hidden mine that could destroy them. By the end of the month, the French supplies were running out. On 31 August, de

A contemporary sketch of Schulenburg's plan of attack against Tournai's western walls. (Public domain)

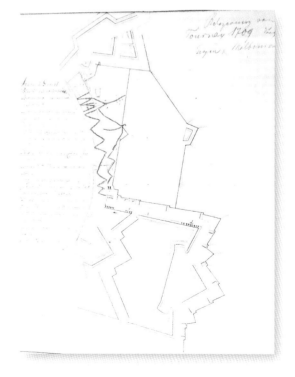

Marlborough and Eugene overseeing the siege of Tournai. The town surrendered on 30 July, the citadel on 3 September. (Musée des Armes et de l'Histoire Militaire, Tournai; author's photograph)

Surville-Hautfort asked for terms. The Allies formally occupied the citadel on 3 September, and the French defenders were granted the honours of war.

The surrender of Tournai citadel dashed Villars' hope that the siege would keep the Allies occupied until the end of the campaign season. He was furious, blaming de Surville-Hautfort for not properly marshalling his supplies. In a series of letters, he branded de Surville-Hautfort 'an idiot' for not ensuring the citadel had a good three months' worth of supplies. 'If this citadel had been supplied as ordered, certainly, without being committed to a battle, we would have reached the end of September and presumably the end of the campaign' (Villars, 1 September 1709). In another letter, he called the surrender of Tournai 'the most shameful thing in the world'.

Villars' had pinned his hopes on Tournai holding out much longer. With only a meagre garrison against two combined Allied armies, de Surville-Hautfort had conducted an active and valiant defence without any hope of reinforcement. It is hard to see what more he could have done, given France's chronic lack of supplies at the time. The Allied victory had cost them over 5,000 casualties – proof of the vigorous French defence.

The fall of Tournai changed the strategic situation. Although the campaign season was well advanced, the initiative was now with the Allies, and, with their customary alacrity, Marlborough and Eugene seized the opportunity.

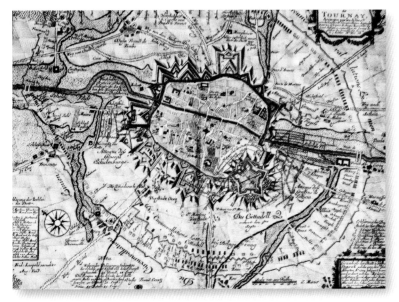

An overview of the Allied siege lines around Tournai. (Musée des Armes et de l'Histoire Militaire, Tournai)

THE ADVANCE ON MONS

The Allies wasted no time at Tournai. They had two viable options open to them: move west to take Ypres and then bypass the Lines of La Bassée to the west, or move on Mons to the east. Ypres was well fortified and reasonably well garrisoned. Mons, however, was only lightly defended by nine understrength Spanish battalions – the remnants of the army of the Spanish Netherlands – supported by two battalions of Bavarians and some dragoons. Mons would be relatively easy to take, and when it fell, most of the Spanish Netherlands would be under Allied control.

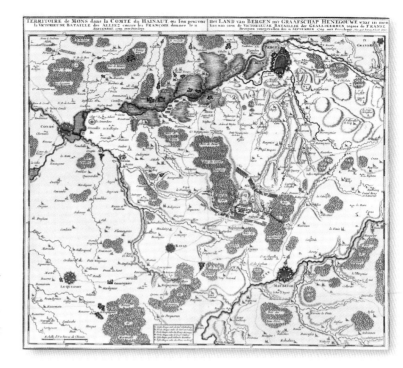

A contemporary map of the Malplaquet campaign area, showing the key fortified towns in red and the deployment of troops at the start of the battle. (Pieter Schenk, c. 1720)

Furthermore, its capture would place the Allies on the far right of the French Lines of La Bassée, in a good position to break through into France. Villars would be forced to move from his entrenchments and offer battle, if he wanted to stop them. Therefore, Marlborough and Eugene decided to move rapidly on Mons.

As Tournai's surrender was still being negotiated, Marlborough sent the Earl of Orkney with a force of grenadiers and cavalry to probe Mons' defences. The artillery and heavy baggage were withdrawn to Brussels, from where they would have a good road to move on Mons. The Prince of Hesse-Kassel with 60 squadrons of cavalry, supported by several battalions of foot, also moved on Mons. He saw off a screen of French dragoons and sorties from the garrison to occupy the outskirts of the town. Hesse-Kassel was backed up by another 40 squadrons of cavalry led by Earl Cadogan.

Villars had barely had time to get over his anger at the fall of Tournai when he learned that the Allies were advancing rapidly on Mons. This seems to have taken him by surprise. He perhaps had thought that the Allies would have turned on Ypres after Tournai, as he knew that was one of their strategic targets. If they had, then a siege there would certainly have kept them occupied to the end of the campaign season. Villars had to act fast and risk battle to stop a potential Allied breakthrough into France around the eastern flank of his lines. He wrote to King Louis, proposing offensive action. The king's reply was: 'Should Mons suffer the same fate as Tournai, our cause is undone. You are by every means in your power to relieve the garrison. The cost is not to be considered.'

Therefore, Villars reinforced the Mons garrison and marched his army from their fortified lines to the east in order to disrupt the Allied siege and block any move south from Mons into France. He sent Christian-Louis, Chevalier de Luxembourg, ahead with 30 squadrons of cavalry, supported by the foot of the Picardie brigade, to intercept the Allied advance guard

39

The approach to battle, 6–10 September 1709

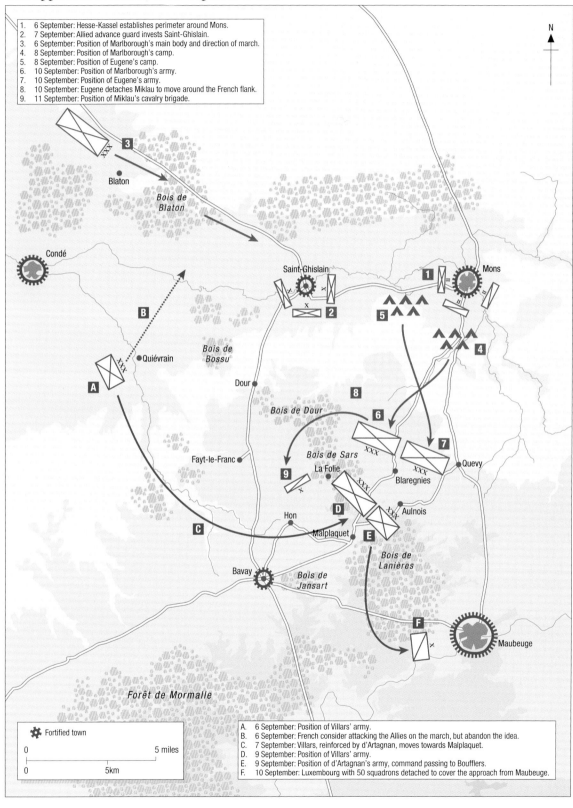

1. 6 September: Hesse-Kassel establishes perimeter around Mons.
2. 7 September: Allied advance guard invests Saint-Ghislain.
3. 6 September: Position of Marlborough's main body and direction of march.
4. 8 September: Position of Marlborough's camp.
5. 8 September: Position of Eugene's camp.
6. 10 September: Position of Marlborough's army.
7. 10 September: Position of Eugene's army.
8. 10 September: Eugene detaches Miklau to move around the French flank.
9. 11 September: Position of Miklau's cavalry brigade.

N

Blaton

Bois de Blaton

Condé

Saint-Ghislain

Mons

Bois de Bossu

Quiévrain

Dour

Bois de Dour

Fayt-le-Franc

Bois de Sars

La Folie

Blaregnies

Quevy

Hon

Aulnois

Malplaquet

Bois de Lanières

Bavay

Bois de Jansart

Forêt de Mormalle

Maubeuge

⚙ Fortified town

0		5 miles
0	5km	

A. 6 September: Position of Villars' army.
B. 6 September: French consider attacking the Allies on the march, but abandon the idea.
C. 7 September: Villars, reinforced by d'Artagnan, moves towards Malplaquet.
D. 9 September: Position of Villars' army.
E. 9 September: Position of d'Artagnan's army, command passing to Boufflers.
F. 10 September: Luxembourg with 50 squadrons detached to cover the approach from Maubeuge.

In 1709, Tournai was one of the best-fortified towns in Flanders. Very little remains today. This tower is a remnant of the original medieval walls, which were incorporated into the 17th/18th-century defences. (Author's photo)

before it could establish itself in siege lines around Mons. Advancing from the south on 5 September, Luxembourg's men skirmished with Hesse-Kassel's troopers, but when he realized the strength of the Allied advance guard, he prudently withdrew.

On 6 September, Villars was encamped at Quiévrain, 20km south-west of Mons, with most of his cavalry and about half of his infantry. The Allies had invested Saint-Ghislain, 11km west of Mons, while Hesse-Kassel had established a perimeter around Mons as Marlborough and Eugene were advancing with their main bodies on separate axes towards the town.

There was an opportunity for the French at this point. Villars considered attacking while the Allies were still strung out, but in a letter to Louis XIV on 6 September, he explained that he dared not risk a battle at this point with his forces as yet unconsolidated. D'Artagnan arrived the following day with the rest of the army, but adequate supplies were still lacking. By 8 September, Marlborough and Eugene were both established outside Mons – Marlborough to the south-west, and Eugene to the west. The French opportunity to attack the Allies on the march had passed.

Ten kilometres south of Mons there is a 3km gap between two woods north of the hamlet of Malplaquet. It was here where Villars led his army. The position was well placed for him to move north in order to disrupt the Allied siege lines, and also provided an excellent defensive position for him to fall back on. On the left of the gap was the dense Bois de Sars, on the right the Bois de Lanières. The smaller Bois de Thierry divided the gap in

A siege mortar and bomb from Tournai. Mortars lobbed explosive bombs over the walls of a besieged city. They were occasionally used in the field. Marlborough deployed three howitzers or mortars at Malplaquet. The terms were used interchangeably but when mounted on field carriages such indirect fire weapons tended to be called 'howitzers'. (Musée des Armes et de l'Histoire Militaire, Tournai)

half, with the Blairon Farm at its southern end. Several small streams running south to north channelized the gap in several places.

Villars marched his army to the Malplaquet gap in the early hours of 9 September, arriving without the Allies being aware of his move until a Dutch cavalry detachment reported it. Marlborough and Eugene, accompanied by 30 squadrons and 400 grenadiers under the command of the Dutch Prince d'Auvergne, moved south towards the Bois de Sars to observe the situation in the morning of 9 September. A skirmish between cavalry piquets ensued, and d'Auvergne led his detachment into the fray. Forced back by superior numbers, d'Auvergne reported the arrival of the full French army into the Malplaquet gap.

At this point, Marlborough and Eugene's armies were encamped outside Mons, about 3km apart. Many of their troops were dispersed – completely unaware of the French move. Joseph Sevin, Chevalier de Quincy, commanding the lead battalion of one of the French columns, recounted in his memoirs: 'We arrived at 10 a.m. [9 September] at the two debouches of Malplaquet without the enemy being informed in any manner of our march on them. All their cavalry was out foraging and the infantry marauding.'

It was one of the very rare occasions when the French had stolen a march on Marlborough. He immediately redeployed his army to face the north end of the Malplaquet gap, calling on Eugene to join him. By 3 p.m., Marlborough's troops were in position, but they were alone.

Blairon Farm divided the gap in half. This view is from the west looking east, from a position just in front of where the French redans stood. (Author's photo)

The army of Prince Eugene, who in the uncertainty of the enemy plan had still not moved, received orders to join the right of Milord the Duke, but rain and obscurity of the night resulted in that [Eugene] did not join until the following day [10 September]. (Dutch archives)

Villars had begun to advance north up the gap, but as Marlborough deployed, he pulled back to adopt a defensive position, his infantry digging in as his artillery engaged the enemy at long range. Had he pressed his attack on 9 September, as Marlborough was redeploying and not yet supported by Eugene, he may well have won a decisive victory.

Many of the participants in the battle (on both sides) recounted in their memoirs that Villars missed a golden opportunity to defeat the Allies piecemeal by not attacking Marlborough on 9 September:

> This attack was the right game and would have been far more embarrassing. (Schulenburg)
>
> [The French generals] remained irresolute ... One knew that only a part of the enemy army [was in position]. It would have been entirely undone had one attacked it. (Chevalier des Bournays)
>
> All our army had arrived when the head of the enemy began to appear ... We did not profit from the most beautiful opportunity in the world to attack them in their march and in detail ... If one had attacked them on the 9th, the day that they arrived, there would have been no more question about their army. It was almost all deployed foraging or marauding and knew nothing of our march until we arrived in range of them. (Chevalier de Foland)

So why did Villars not attack when he had the chance? He was by nature an aggressive commander. That he did not attack from Quiévrain on 6 September is perfectly understandable, as his army was not yet in place and lacked supplies. That he had seized the initiative by marching to the Malplaquet gap and then stopped when the Allied armies were separated and caught off guard is much harder to understand. The most likely

French soldiers on the march at the time of the Malplaquet campaign. This copy of an original by Jean-Antoine Watteau gives a realistic impression of Villars' army – a far cry from modern march discipline. (De Agostini/ Getty Images)

This plan of the battle and troop deployments at Malplaquet by Isaac van der Kloot was printed in 1729. It provides the Allied order of battle at the bottom. (*Histoire militaire du Prince Eugène de Savoie*)

explanation is that Villars knew that to risk an attack was to risk the only army France had left in the north – attack being a riskier proposition than defence. Despite his best efforts, his units were still understrength, underfed and undersupplied. Furthermore, on every occasion his men had met Marlborough in battle, they had been soundly defeated. He had forced the enemy onto ground of his choosing, and it was perfect for a defensive battle. With his flanks well protected by two woods, he could easily hold the 3km-wide gap and force the enemy to throw themselves at him. The odds on winning a defensive battle on such favourable terrain seemed much greater than risking an attack, even though this gave the Allies the chance to bring their armies together and retake the initiative. Being only 10km south of Mons, they could not ignore the French army without abandoning their attempt to take the town, and it was too late in the season for them to shift their advance to Ypres or elsewhere to the west.

Villars began to entrench his infantry to cover the gap and the edges of the woods that defined it. He sent the Chevalier de Luxembourg with 50 squadrons of horse to cover any attempt by the Allies to flank the French right (east), which was only guarded by the lightly held town of Maubeuge.

Marlborough observed the French preparations as they dug their entrenchments across the gap. Eighteen battalions were left behind at Mons as the main Allied forces converged on the north end of the Malplaquet gap. Eugene's army began arriving in the evening of 9 September, and the Allies considered attacking the following day before the French fieldworks could be too far advanced. Twenty battalions and ten squadrons under Henry Withers were marching from Tournai, but they were not expected to arrive before 11 September. Much of the artillery was still on its way from Brussels, and would not be in position to support an attack until later on 10 September. Furthermore, the Allies had not yet had the chance to fully reconnoitre the ground. They could see that the gap was cut by streams and boggy ground, but had not had the time to determine where an attack might be feasible. 'Since we do not know the ground we dare not take any risks. The terrain is very uneven' (Prince Eugene).

Therefore, the Allied council of war decided that an attack on 10 September was not feasible. Even though a delay would allow the French to further improve their defences, it was judged more prudent to wait for the artillery and Withers' reinforcements, using the time to conduct a proper reconnaissance of the ground.

The stage was set for the Battle of Malplaquet to take place on 11 September 1709.

ORDERS OF BATTLE, MALPLAQUET

Piecing together definitive orders of battle for Malplaquet is a complex task. Various national archives give fairly comprehensive lists of troops in their static camps, the French from July 1709 and the Allies from June. Formal brigades, divisions and corps did not exist in the early 1700s. Units were frequently switched from one commander to another, sometimes on the day of battle. Archival lists from several months before the battle have to be cross-referenced with regimental histories and personal accounts of the men who fought at Malplaquet.

Some of what follows is fairly certain – most notably the deployment of the French and Dutch foot and Schulenburg's Imperialists. The exact placement of the British, Prussian, Hanoverian and other German foot (split between Orkney, Rantzau, Fink, Lottum, Gauvin and Withers) is more difficult. This is compounded by the fact that some units known to have been involved in the campaign remained behind at Tournai, while others were besieging Mons. Regimental histories have helped to identify some units that were present at Tournai or Mons, but not at Malplaquet, and vice versa.

Determining the exact deployment of the horse and dragoons is even more problematic. This is not helped by the fact that a cavalry regiment could have its squadrons deployed in different places. The list that follows, therefore, does not give the designation of every squadron from every regiment. Rather it indicates the total number of squadrons under a specific general, indicating nationality and type.

The French army: 120 battalions, 260 squadrons, 80 guns

French archives identify 118 battalions of foot on the battlefield, but if two 'battalions' of the Royal Artillery are added, then the numbers tally. The exact numbers of horse and dragoons are more difficult. Although the deployment of the Maison du Roi, Gendarmes, Carabiniers and Dragoons are fairly certain, there are no primary sources that give the location of any of the more numerous *chevaux-légers*. It may have been that Luxembourg's reserve was not on the battlefield, as it had earlier been sent off to the far right to protect the approaches from Maubeuge, and there are no definitive accounts of it returning.

FRENCH RIGHT WING (DUC DE BOUFFLERS)

COMTE D'ARTAGNAN

(commanding 30 battalions on the far right)
La Marck (at the north end of the Bois de Lanières)
Battalion of converged grenadiers
Chateauneuf (one battalion)
La Marck (two battalions)
Sebret (behind La Marck)
Perche (two battalions)
Foix (two battalions)
Santerre (two battalions)
de la Motte (behind Sebret)
Touraine (two battalions)
La Fère (two battalions)
Montroux (one battalion)
Agénois (two battalions)
de Beuil (holding the far-right entrenchments)
Piquets (skirmishers detached from various battalions as a screen)
Bourbonnais (two battalions)
Piedmont (three battalions)
de Guiche (holding the entrenchments to the left of de Beuil)
Bourgogne (two battalions)
Royal Italien (Italians) (one battalion)
Boulonnais (two battalions)
Royal (three battalions)

MARQUIS D'HAUTEFORT

(commanding the reserve of 16 battalions on the right)
Mortemart
Mortemart (two battalions)
Mouchy
Lorraine (two battalions)
Navarre (three battalions)
Nice (one battalion)

May
May (three battalions, Swiss)
Greder Suisse (two battalions, Swiss)
Brendele (three battalions, Swiss)

HENRI DE STECKEMBERG

(commanding 12 battalions holding the centre of the entrenchments)
Alsace (four battalions)
Lannoy (two battalions)
Picardie (three battalions)
Royal Roussillon (two battalions)
Deslandes (one battalion)

CHARLES, DUC DE MONTBASSON

(commanding the six battalions of guards holding the left of the entrenchments)
Gardes Françaises (four battalions)
Gardes Suisses (two battalions)

HORSE

Maison du Roi
13 squadrons; on the left behind Montbasson
Chevalier de Luxembourg
50 squadrons *chevaux-légers*; held in reserve, or perhaps still to the east of the battlefield

ARTILLERY

One massed battery of 20 guns in enfilade between Steckemberg and d'Artagnan
One battery of six guns in front of de Beuil's brigade
Ten guns dispersed along the front

FRENCH LEFT WING (DUC DE VILLARS)

COMTE DE CHEMERAULT

(commanding 17 battalions of foot in and behind the redans)
O'Brien (Irish; in the right redans)
O'Donnell (one battalion)
Galmoy (one battalion)
Dorington (one battalion)
O'Brien (one battalion)
Lee (one battalion)
Seignelay (French; in the left redans)
Champagne (three battalions)
Louvigny (two battalions)
Béarn (two battalions)
Isenghien (one battalion)

Mercy/de la Colonie (German; in reserve, to the right rear of the Irish)
Gardes de Bavière (two battalions)
Gardes de Cologne (two battalions)

COMTE D'ALBERGOTTI

(commanding 21 battalions In the Bois de Sars)
d'Angennes (occupying the south end of the woods, facing east where Lottum attacked)
La Reine (three battalions)
Boufflers (one battalion)
La Sarre (one battalion)
Royal la Marine (two battalions)

Charost (two battalions)
Sparre (two battalions)
Goesbriant (occupying the north edge of the woods, where Schulenburg attacked)
Le Roy (four battalions)
Saintonge (two battalions)
Bretagne (two battalions)
Provence (two battalions)

MARQUIS DE PUYSÉGUR

(commanding 12 battalions on the far left, facing the south edge of the Bois de Sars)
Mouy
Gondrin (two battalions)
Greder Allemand (two battalions, Germans)
Luxembourg (two battalions)
Mancis
Guyenne (two battalions)
Poitou (two battalions)
Arling
Chartres (two battalions)

CHEVALIER DE CROY

(commanding a reserve of five battalions to the rear of Arling, on the left)
Tourville (two battalions)
Perrin (two battalions)
Croy (one battalion)

HORSE

(143 squadrons in four divisions)
Dauger
On the right in three lines, with eight squadrons of Gendarmes in front.
de la Vallière
In the centre behind the redans, in two lines.
Wozel
Behind the Bois de Sars, in two lines
Broglie
On the far left, in two lines with ten squadrons of Carabiniers in front

DRAGOONS

Comte de Villars
Reserve of 18 regiments (54 squadrons – in reserve on the far left)

ARTILLERY

One battery of 20 guns (to the front right of the redans)
One battery of five guns (in front of the centre redans)
One battery of four guns (to the front left of the redans)
One battery of five guns (on the north edge of the Bois de Sars)
Ten guns (dispersed along the front)

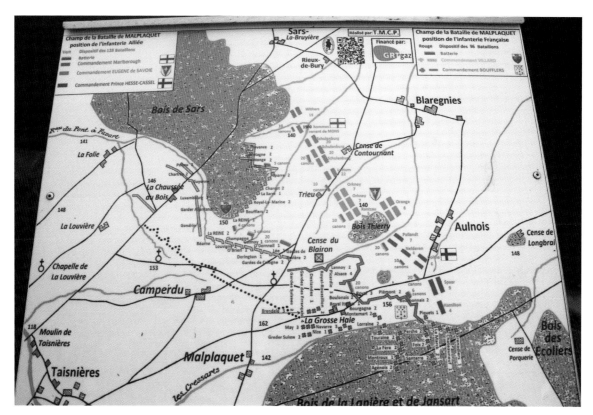

One of several modern maps displayed on the Malplaquet battlefield. This one shows the deployment of troops at the start of the battle. The French order of battle is based on a combination of camp records from July 1709 and accounts of French officers. (Author's photo)

The Allied army: 129 battalions, 253 squadrons, 101 guns

As with the French, the numbers of battalions are fairly certain, the squadrons of cavalry less so.

ALLIED RIGHT WING (PRINCE EUGENE)

LIEUTENANT-GENERAL HENRY WITHERS

(commanding 19 battalions from Tournai, assisted by major-generals Temple and Hohendorf)
Ingoldsby[1] (British)
Lalo (British)
Primrose (British)
Prince Georg (Danish)
Donep (Danish)
Sponeck (Danish)
Pretorius (Danish)
Grothusen (Holstein-Gottorf)
Dobrokowsky (Holstein-Gottorf)
Pfalz Grenadier Guards
2nd Battalion, Saxe-Meiningen (Pfalz)
Nassau-Dillenburg (Pfalz)
Haxthausen (Pfalz)
Freudenberg (Pfalz)
Lemsberg (Munster)
Düren (Munster)
Prince Wilhelm (Hesse-Kassel)
Two battalions (Würtemberg grenadiers)

MAJOR-GENERAL MIKLAU[2]

20 squadrons of Saxon and Hessian cavalry and Imperial hussars (on the far-right flank)

BRIGADIER GAUVAIN

(commanding 1,900 men arriving from Mons)
This was most likely an ad hoc force drawn from the 18 battalions holding the siege lines at Mons. Gauvain was Hanoverian, and it is likely (but far from certain) that the 1,900 men were drawn from the following Hanoverian battalions which were at Mons and Malplaquet, but not accounted for elsewhere:
Gauvain
du Breuil
de Luer
Costeritz
Tecklenburg

REICHSGRAF VON DER SCHULENBURG

40 battalions in three lines that attacked the north end of the Bois de Sars. The composition of this force is the most certain of all the Allied contingents, thanks to Schulenburg's first-hand account.

First Line

(lieutenant-generals Graf von Wackerbarth [Saxon] and von Harrach [Austrian] commanding; major-generals von Canitz [in Saxon service], Fechenbach [Austrian] and van der Beck [Dutch] assisting)
First battalion, Thungen (Austria)
First battalion, Baden (Austria)
Grenadiers (Hesse-Kassel)
Ernefeld (Munster)
Cavagnac (Ansbach)
Carl Rex (or Carlis) (Walloons)
Hercules (Holstein-Gottorf)
Württemberg (Danish)
Wilke (Hesse-Kassel)
Two battalions of Saxon foot guards
One battalion of Danish foot guards

Second Line

(Lieutenant-General von Friesheim [in Dutch service] commanding; major-generals Landsburg [Dutch], von Zobel and von Sacken [Hessian] assisting)
Second battalion, Thungen (Austria)
Lubeck (Pfalz)
Iselbach (Pfalz)
Erbprinz August Wilhelm (Braunschweig-Wolfenbüttel)
Castell (Ansbach)
Herrmann (Württemberg)
Exterde (Hesse-Kassel)
Baumbach (Hesse-Kassel)
Fürstenburg (Saxony)
Kurprinz (Saxony)
Weissenfels (Saxony)
Bielke (Denmark)

Third Line

(Lieutenant-General von Bettendorf [in Pfalz service], commanding; major-generals von Sternfels [in Württemberg service] and von Schwärzel [in Danish service] assisting)
Second battalion, Baden (Austria)
Dalberg (Würzburg)
Deaston (Würzburg)
Sachsen-Meiningen (Pfalz)
Sulzbach (Pfalz)
Bevern (Braunschweig-Wolfenbüttel)
Flohs (Mecklenburg)
Delsuperche (Walloons in Dutch service)
Maximilian (Hesse-Kassel)
Erbprinz von Hessen-Kassel (Hesse-Kassel)
Stockerath (Hesse-Kassel)
Sternfels (Württemberg)
Wackerbarth (Saxony)
Ogilvy (Saxony)
Boisset (Denmark)
Schwärzel (Denmark)

WÜRTTEMBERG-NEUENSTADT

81 squadrons of Imperial and Danish horse, dragoons and hussars. Held in reserve to the rear of Schulenburg.

---

1   Only Ingoldsby's Battalion (Royal Irish) is certain. They were brigaded with Lalo and Primrose according to a list in the Imperial archives for June 1709. The other battalions are those known to have been part of Eugene's command at Malplaquet, but were not with Schulenburg. The third battalion Dutch Gardes te Voet were originally part of this command, but they moved over to the left flank to join their compatriots.

2   Miklau originally had five squadrons, but according to Schulenburg he was later reinforced by an additional ten squadrons drawn from the Imperial cavalry division. Wackerbarth says that Miklau ended up with 20 squadrons. That some hussars were present comes from de Rozel's account of the fight between his carabiniers and Miklau's detachment.

ALLIED CENTRE (DUKE OF MARLBOROUGH)

REICHSGRAF VON WYLICH UND LOTTUM

22 battalions in three lines that attacked the east face of the Bois de Sars. Argyle (English) commanding eight battalions in the first line; Webb (English) commanding eight battalions in the second line; von Tettau and von Denhoff (Prussian) commanding six battalions in the third line. The dispositions of the lines is not known, but the likely overall composition is as follows:

14 battalions (Prussians)
Füsiliergarde
Leibregiment (two battalions)
Kronprinz (three battalions)
Prince Albrecht (two battalions)
Lottum (two battalions)
Dünhoff
Erbprinz von Hessen-Kassel
Anhalt-Zerbst
du Troussel
Five battalions (English)
Argyle
Webb
Temple
Godfrey
Evans
Three battalions (Hanoverians)
Melleville (or Malfyl)
Gohr
Diepenbroick (or Dieffenbruch)

EARL OF ORKNEY

Nine battalions (English – holding the right of centre)
1st Guards (Grenadier)
2nd Guards (Coldstream), later sent to reinforce Lottum
Orkney (Royal Scots), later sent to reinforce Lottum
North and Grey (this was a single person: the Baron of North and Grey)
Howe
Erle
Sabine
Meredith
Orrery

REICHSGRAF FINCK VON FINCKENSTEIN

Four battalions to the left of Orkney. The composition of this force is tentative. It certainly contained Prussians. Preston and Pendergast's English were brigaded with the Prussians in June 1709, and Pendergast's regiment is recorded engaging the French Gendarmes from the eastern redans, which Finck occupied. In many British accounts, Finck's command is incorporated into Orkney's numbers. Finck and Orkney were of equal rank (lieutenant-generals) and were separate divisions. It may be that up to two of the English battalions listed under Orkney above were actually under Finck's command.
Alt Dohna (Prussian)
Jung Dohna (Prussian)
Preston (English)
Pendergast (English)

MAJOR-GENERAL RANTZAU

Four battalions of Hanoverians, to the left rear of Finck
Rantzau (two battalions)
Stallmeister
Belling

CAVALRY

d'Auvergne
62 squadrons of Dutch horse and dragoons, in three lines deployed behind Orkney
Von Bülow
54 squadrons of Hanoverian and Prussian horse and dragoons, in three lines to the left of d'Auvergne
Wood
15 squadrons of British horse and dragoons, in two lines, covering to the rear of d'Auvergne, and von Bülow and the gap between them

ARTILLERY

40 guns supporting Lottum's attack
Three mortars or howitzers, and ten guns to the right of Orkney
28 guns to the left of Orkney

ALLIED LEFT WING (GRAAF VAN TILLY)

PRINCE OF ORANGE

17 battalions of Dutch, on the right, in two lines
Pallandt (right)
Oranje-Frieslande (two battalions)
Zoutland
Van der Beek
May (two battalions, Swiss)
Heukelom
Van Welderen (centre)
Schmid (two battalions, Swiss)
Welderen
Yvoy
de Dohna and Van Heyden (left)
Stürler (two battalions, Swiss)
Hüffel
Veglin
Heyden
Nassau-Wondenburg

BARON FAGEL

13 battalions of Dutch, on the far left, in two lines

Spaar and Oxenstiern (right)
2nd and 3rd battalions Gardes te Voet; the 1st battalion joined later
Rechteren (centre)
Fournier (Walloons)
Dohna-Ferrassieré (Swiss)
Berkhoffer
Keppel
Oxenstierna (Swedes)
1st battalion Mestral (Swiss)
Hamilton (left)
Tullibardine (Scots)
Hepburn (Scots)
2nd battalion Mestral (Swiss)
Pallandt

PRINCE OF HESSE-KASSEL

21 squadrons of Dutch horse, behind Orange

ARTILLERY

20 guns in front of Fagel, on the far left

THE BATTLE OF MALPLAQUET

THE FRENCH DEPLOYMENT

Our position was a peculiar one but advantageous nevertheless. On our front lay these two woods [Sars to the west, Lanières to the east] separate the one from the other, forming a kind of broad avenue wide enough for 20 battalions to pass formed up side by side, which opened up onto the plain we were occupying. Maréchal de Villars ordered the infantry to occupy the end of this avenue and the edges of the woods so as to create a sort of blind alley and to prevent entrance to the plain. The cavalry remained on the plain, the Maison du Roi in the centre – in the rear of the infantry posted across the alley – the rest on the right and left of our line in rear of the woods. (Jean-Martin de la Colonie, commander of the Bavarian and Cologne troops in the French army)

Blairon (today often written Bléron) was not incorporated into the French defences, but it is likely that some skirmishers were sent forward to occupy it and hinder the Dutch attack on the eastern flank. (Author's photo)

While his artillery and cavalry piquets kept Allied reconnaissance patrols at bay, Villars' infantry began to dig in. The gap (or avenue, to use de la Colonie's term) was bisected by several south–north running streams and the Rue des Trieux, which ran from Mons in the north, through the French lines to the hamlet of Malplaquet and beyond. This road marked the division between Villars' command on the left and Boufflers' on the right. The Bois de Thierry, a few hundred metres to the east of the road, divided the gap in two almost equal halves. A stream ran along the eastern edge of the woods, with Blairon Farm just to the south. The Bois de Thierry, Blairon Farm and the stream provided a significant barrier almost exactly halfway along the gap. This would force the Allies to split their attack in two, making it difficult to switch troops from one side to the other.

To the west of the Rue des Trieux, the French constructed a series of redans – v-shaped earthworks with ditches and a firing parapet. These redans were infantry strongpoints with sufficient gaps between them to allow cavalry to pass through, should the French wish to launch a mounted counter-attack.

There were probably nine of these, although a number of modern historians give lower numbers, ranging from five to eight. Earlier accounts, and most of the French ones, say that there were nine. That there may have been fewer is reinforced by de la Colonie's account that his Bavarians had no cover from Allied artillery fire on 10 September, and that they only moved into the redans later on the day of battle after the Irish Brigade had vacated the ones they had been occupying. It may be that nine were planned, but some of those on the right had not been completed before battle commenced.

The eastern half of the gap was covered by a continuous line of entrenchments that doubled back on themselves, before extending out to the Bois de Lanières. This created a re-entrant where Saint-Hilaire concealed a 20-gun battery that could give enfilade fire on any attack.

The French occupied the edges of both the Bois de Sars and Bois de Lanières, in both cases fortifying their positions with abatis – entanglements formed by felled trees and sharpened stakes. The Bois de Sars was held by 21 battalions commanded by the Comte d'Albergotti. The Comte d'Artagnan deployed 17 battalions in the Bois de Lanières, including a battalion of grenadiers drawn from several line regiments and posted on the northern edge of the woods. Thirty-one battalions occupied the entrenchments on the eastern half of the gap, with the Gardes Suisses and Gardes Françaises on the left. Another 16 battalions were held in reserve. On the western half of the gap, 17 battalions under the Comte de Chemerault occupied the redans in the centre. Of these, de la Colonie's four German battalions were initially outside the protection of the redans. Another 17 battalions were entrenched to the south of the Bois de Sars on the far French left, commanded by the Marquis de Puységur and the Chevalier de Croy.

Most of the French horse were drawn up in long lines on the plain behind the redans and the Bois de Sars – the Maison du Roi and Gendarmes on the right, Carabiniers on the left. There was not much room for mounted action, but cavalry could attack through the gaps in the redans or counter any Allied breakthrough in the centre. A large brigade of dragoons (18 regiments/54 squadrons) was posted in reserve on the left to the south of the Bois de Sars. The Chevalier de Luxembourg had 50 squadrons of horse that had been sent off to guard the approaches to the French right. It is not clear whether or not they were on the actual field of battle on 11 September, but if they were, then they would have been held in reserve on the right.

The French had 80 guns. Saint-Hilaire deployed most of these in large batteries, situated where they would cause maximum damage on the possible attack routes. Twenty were hidden in the enfilade position on the eastern half of the gap with another ten guns deployed on the far right of the entrenchments. Six of these were in the entrenchments, the other four placed to cover the edge of the Bois de Lanières. Forty guns were deployed in three batteries covering the left, centre and right of the redans, and five

A portrait of Antoine de la Roque, a French soldier who had one of his legs amputated below the knee after it was shattered by a cannonball at Malplaquet. Sketched in 1710 by Jean-Antoine Watteau. (The Print Collector/Getty Images)

(Schulenburg says six) were set up on the edge of the Bois de Sars facing north. The remaining pieces were most probably distributed amongst the front-line battalions. We do not know the calibre of these guns, but it is likely that those deployed in the massed batteries were typical 6-pounder field guns while those distributed along the line, and probably those in the Bois de Sars, were more likely to have been light 3-pounders.

THE ALLIED DEPLOYMENT

The Allied heavy guns arrived from Brussels on 10 September, and by 3 p.m. enough were in place to begin a long-range bombardment of the French positions in the gap. The French artillery replied in kind. That afternoon, Saint-Ghislain was captured by the Allies, releasing more troops to join the main army. Leaving 12 battalions to garrison Tournai and two others to garrison Lille, Lieutenant-General Henry Withers was on his way with 20 battalions from Tournai. Eighteen battalions were left to maintain the siege lines around Mons, although 1,900 men (drawn from several battalions) were led south by the Hanoverian Brigadier Gauvin (or Gouvain) to reinforce Eugene.

The Allied generals could see that the French were turning the gap between the two woods into a deadly killing ground. De la Colonie had remarked that 'the enemy could only attack us by advancing up this avenue'. Marlborough and Eugene saw another possibility. Their plan was to hold in the centre while launching attacks on both wings. These might succeed in turning a flank, or cause the French to draw troops from the centre to reinforce the wings, which would then make an attack in the centre feasible.

Prince Eugene commanded the right, with 40 battalions under Reichsgraf von der Schulenburg poised to attack the north-east corner of the Bois de Sars. This was a composite force of Imperialists bolstered by Danish, Walloon and German subsidiary troops in the pay of the Maritime Powers. Thirty battalions of Graaf van Tilly's Dutch army (including Swiss, Swedes and Scots) would attack through the eastern half of the gap to the Bois de Lanières. Tilly would take little or no part in the action, leaving active command of the Dutch attack to the young Prince of Orange. As the attacks went in on the wings, the centre would be held by a thin line of 17 battalions of British, Prussians and Hanoverians under lieutenant-generals Orkney (British) and Finck (Prussian), and Major-General Rantzau (Danish, commanding Hanoverians).

This scene from Lock's *Illustrated History of the World* shows the Duke of Marlborough surveying the French positions at Malplaquet on 9 September. D'Auvergne's Dutch cavalry are behind him, the Mill of Sars in the background. (Universal History Archive/Universal Images Group via Getty Images)

As Schulenburg's attack went in on the north-eastern edge of the Bois de Sars, the Prussian Reichsgraf von Wylich und Lottum would lead 22 battalions of Prussians and British towards the French redans in the centre, and then swing to the right to attack the southern half of the eastern edge of the Bois de Sars.

Most of the Allied cavalry were held in reserve behind the foot in the centre. They would be ready to counter any French horse that might push through the gaps in the redans, and to exploit any success by the Allied foot. This central cavalry reserve was deployed in three divisions: the Prince d'Auvergne's Dutch in three lines on the western half of the gap, with von Bülow and Wood's Germans and British to their left. Württemberg's Imperial and Danish cavalry were held back behind d'Auvergne's right.

Twenty-one squadrons of Dutch horse, commanded by the Prince of Hesse-Kassel, were deployed on the left behind the Dutch foot to support their attack. A brigade of five squadrons of (mostly Hessians) under Major-General Miklau was detached from the Imperial cavalry to work its way around the west of the Bois de Sars, to come out on the French left flank. Fearing that Miklau's brigade was too small, Eugene was persuaded by his generals to detach a further ten squadrons from Württemberg's cavalry to bolster them, although Wackerbarth, one of Schulenburg's lieutenant-generals, says that Miklau ended up with a total of 20 squadrons.

Withers' 20 battalions from Tournai arrived at 6 a.m. on the day of battle, according to most sources. However, Sergeant John Millner, who served in Ingoldsby's Irish battalion that was part of Withers' force, says that they arrived late in the evening of 10 September. The original plan was for them to reinforce the Dutch on the left flank. Marlborough decided there was nothing to be gained by moving Withers across the Allied lines from the right to the far left. Instead, they would work their way along tracks through the Bois de Sars to the right of Schulenburg. The 1st Battalion, Dutch Gardes te Voet was one of Withers' 20 battalions. They did move over to the left flank to join their compatriots, leaving Withers with 19 German, Danish and British battalions.

The Allied attack on the morning of 11 September would see more than 81 battalions attacking the Bois de Sars (Schulenburg's 40, Lottum's 22, Withers'

On the morning of 11 September 1709, the battlefield was covered with a dense fog. This view, in similar circumstances, is taken from the French centre looking north-east towards Blairon and Thierry woods. (Author's photo)

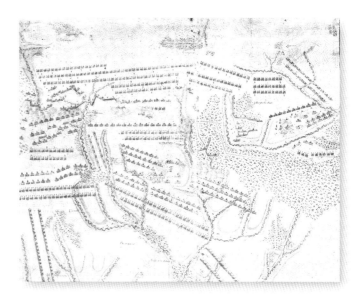

A contemporary German print showing the battlefield and troop dispositions at the start – the Allies at the bottom, the French at the top. (Germanisches Nationalmuseum)

19 and Gauvin's 1,900 men), which was defended by 21 French battalions. On the other flank, 30 Dutch battalions would be attacking 58.

The Allies had 101 guns deployed by late afternoon on 10 September. A grand battery of 40 guns was positioned to fire on the eastern edge of the Bois de Sars to support Lottum's attack. Ten guns and three howitzers (the latter able to fire indirectly) were set up to the right of Orkney in the centre. Firing indirectly, the howitzers were able to drop shells into the redans and onto the lines of horse behind them. A further 28-gun battery was positioned to the left of Orkney, in front of Rantzau's Hanoverians, in the middle of the gap. The remaining 20 guns were set up to support the Dutch attack on the far left. Most of these would have been 6-pounder field guns, but it is quite likely that some heavier 12-pounders, used at the siege of Tournai, formed part of the 40-gun battery supporting Lottum.

In addition to the above, Schulenburg had 12 guns following up behind his foot, which he took through the Bois de Sars then set up on the southern edge to engage the French reserve lines beyond. Taking relatively heavy pieces with horses, limbers and their civilian drivers through the woods with combat going on all around would have taken a major miracle, even if the woodland tracks offered reasonably good going. An Imperial regiment of foot usually included a light 3-pounder gun manned by infantrymen from the battalions. It is most likely that Schulenburg's 12 pieces were these regimental guns taken from their infantry units to form a light battery that followed up behind the infantry attack, probably being manhandled through the tracks in the woods.

THE OPENING SALVO

Throughout the late afternoon and early evening of 10 September, sporadic artillery fire harassed both armies as they made their preparations for battle. The French suffered more from this, as their army was deployed awaiting attack and their men were busy digging ditches and forming earthworks. Most of the Allied troops were held back out of range.

> The Allies, not being in a position to attack us formally on the day of our arrival [9 September] nor on the following day, placed batteries of artillery which opened fire on every point [in the centre] but especially on the Maison du Roi, and as we [the Cologne and Bavarian foot] were posted exactly in front of these, many shots intended for them constantly carried off someone in our brigade. On the afternoon of 10 September, the enemy began to construct a battery about half-way up the avenue, and during the night armed it with 30 cannon [actually 40] of large calibre to breach the entrenchments in the wood on our left [Bois de Sars]. (Jean-Martin de la Colonie)

We do not know how the Allies were able to position their gun batteries without interference from the French. Most probably, they deployed cavalry to cover them, perhaps dismounting some dragoons and backing them up with a few battalions of foot, while keeping most of their troops out of range of the French guns. Quite possibly, Villars felt it preferable to have the Allies place their batteries and commit to a place of attack, rather than risk a battle developing if he attempted to counter them.

During the evening of 10 September, after the guns fell silent, men on both sides (including senior officers) left their positions to fraternize with their opposing numbers.

> Monsieur d'Albergotti in visiting his posts, found those of the enemy so far advanced, said that he was curious to speak with an enemy general officer. Du Sosoir, captain of cavalry who was with him, advanced and made the proposition to the enemy … A moment later, they sent a trumpeter forward to say to Monsieur d'Albergotti that, if he desired, the Prince of Hesse-Kassel and Cadogan were there and would be delighted to speak to him. Strong promises were made on both sides … We embraced, but I noticed that the enemy tried to observe the situation of our infantry in the Bois de Sars which made me uncomfortable. I spoke briskly with one of the officers there. I wanted to make them leave but without success for an hour. (Comte Dauger)

That such fraternization could have taken place may seem strange to modern readers. In the early 18th century, allegiance was to a monarch or paymaster, not to nationality. Men of all European countries fought on both sides. Swiss, Irish, Scots, Germans and Walloons could be found in the ranks of both the French and Allies. There were French exiles in the Dutch army and British in the French army. Men on both sides would have been curious to meet with their counterparts in the opposing army. This fraternization may have been something spontaneous, or perhaps a deliberate attempt on the part of the Allies to scout out the French positions. In all likelihood, it was a combination of both. When Villars became aware, he put a stop to it. 'It was not proper for Cadogan to have the opportunity to observe the disposition on our left and that our trenches would value nothing' (Marquis de la Frézelière).

That Cadogan was involved tends to lend credence to the possibility that the Allies used this opportunity to gain intelligence. Earl Cadogan was Marlborough's quartermaster-general, and had a reputation for spying out enemy positions. As previously noted, in the opening moves of the 1709 campaign, he had infiltrated the Lines of La Bassée, disguised as a peasant, to gather intelligence on the strength of the French defences.

The morning of 11 September dawned with a fog covering the battlefield. As it began to clear, at about 7.30 a.m. (some sources say 7 a.m.), the Allied guns opened fire. This was the signal to commence the attack. Schulenburg and Lottum were to advance immediately on the right, while the Dutch were to launch their attack on the left 30 minutes

This print by Pieter Schenk is one of many such contemporary illustrations of the Battle of Malplaquet. (Rijksmuseum Amsterdam; public domain)

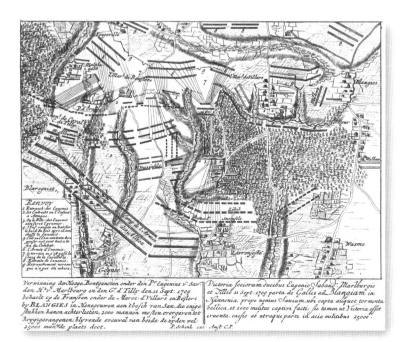

55

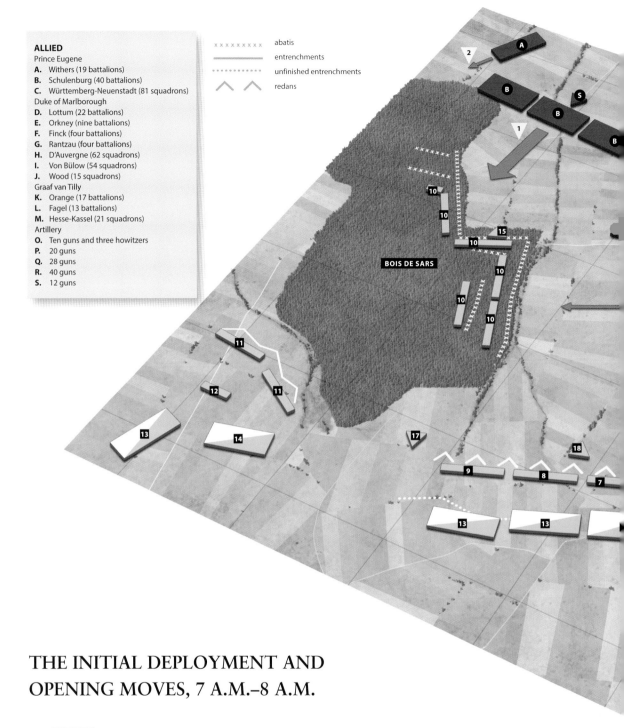

ALLIED

Prince Eugene

A. Withers (19 battalions)
B. Schulenburg (40 battalions)
C. Württemberg-Neuenstadt (81 squadrons)

Duke of Marlborough

D. Lottum (22 battalions)
E. Orkney (nine battalions)
F. Finck (four battalions)
G. Rantzau (four battalions)
H. D'Auvergne (62 squadrons)
I. Von Bülow (54 squadrons)
J. Wood (15 squadrons)

Graaf van Tilly

K. Orange (17 battalions)
L. Fagel (13 battalions)
M. Hesse-Kassel (21 squadrons)

Artillery

O. Ten guns and three howitzers
P. 20 guns
Q. 28 guns
R. 40 guns
S. 12 guns

x x x x x x x x x   abatis
———————   entrenchments
· · · · · · · · · · ·   unfinished entrenchments
⌃ ⌃   redans

BOIS DE SARS

THE INITIAL DEPLOYMENT AND OPENING MOVES, 7 A.M.–8 A.M.

EVENTS

1. Schulenburg attacks the Bois de Sars at 7.30 a.m.
2. Withers advances through the Bois de Sars on the far Allied left.
3. Württemberg-Neuenstadt detaches ten squadrons to reinforce Miklau's flank march.
4. Lottum advances towards the French redans, then turns to the right to attack the Bois de Sars.
5. Orkney detaches two battalions to reinforce Lottum.
6. The Dutch attack the French entrenchments at 8 a.m.
7. Rantzau detaches two battalions to reinforce Orange.

Note: gridlines are shown at intervals of 500m (547 yards)

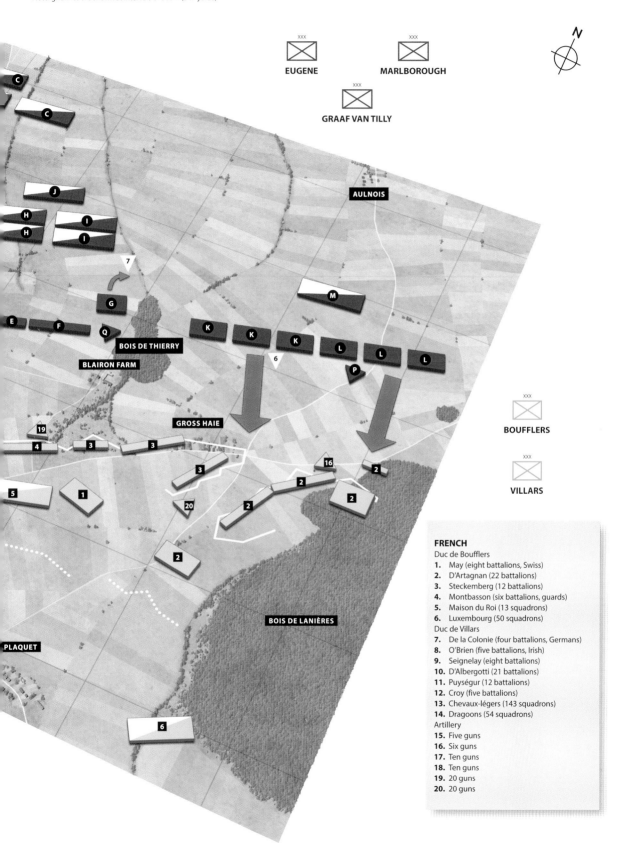

EUGENE

MARLBOROUGH

GRAAF VAN TILLY

AULNOIS

BOIS DE THIERRY

BLAIRON FARM

GROSS HAIE

BOUFFLERS

VILLARS

BOIS DE LANIÈRES

PLAQUET

FRENCH
Duc de Boufflers
1. May (eight battalions, Swiss)
2. D'Artagnan (22 battalions)
3. Steckemberg (12 battalions)
4. Montbasson (six battalions, guards)
5. Maison du Roi (13 squadrons)
6. Luxembourg (50 squadrons)
Duc de Villars
7. De la Colonie (four battalions, Germans)
8. O'Brien (five battalions, Irish)
9. Seignelay (eight battalions)
10. D'Albergotti (21 battalions)
11. Puységur (12 battalions)
12. Croy (five battalions)
13. Chevaux-légers (143 squadrons)
14. Dragoons (54 squadrons)
Artillery
15. Five guns
16. Six guns
17. Ten guns
18. Ten guns
19. 20 guns
20. 20 guns

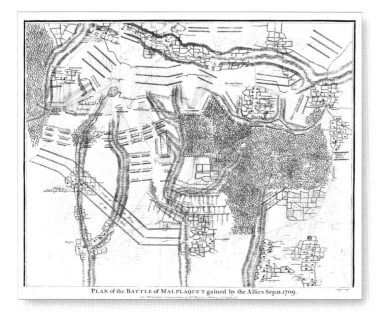

PLAN of the BATTLE of MALPLAQUET gained by the Allies Sep.11.1709.

This near-contemporary engraving of the battle shows the deployment of troops and the artillery angles of fire. (From *The History of England*, by Paul Rapin de Thoyras, 1740)

later. The delay between the two attacks was probably to first fix Villars' attention to one wing, and as he began to formulate his plan of response, to hit the other to keep him off balance. A number of modern accounts say that the Prince of Orange was so anxious for glory that he ignored the 30-minute delay, launching his attack at the same time as Schulenburg. This is not backed up by contemporary reports.

THE BOIS DE SARS

The north-eastern corner of the Bois de Sars had been cut away to form a clearing. This clearing, known today as the Trieu du Bois, was 700m long (north to south) and 300m wide (east to west). Open to the north and east, it was bordered on the west and south by the woods. It was across this cut, and through the woods along the western edge, that Schulenburg's 40 battalions attacked. Two streams presented additional obstacles, and they also made the ground marshy.

Writing the day after the battle, Schulenburg gives a detailed account of the action. 'On the 11th at 4 a.m. after deploying my troops and the 12 artillery pieces, I received my orders from Prince Eugene.' He goes on to say that he arranged his troops in three lines, 'according to their rank and nationality'.

Graf von Wackerbarth arranged the first line, von Friesheim the second and von Bettendorf the third. The best troops – senior Austrian regiments, converged Hessian grenadiers, Saxon and Danish guards – formed the first line. Once the lines were deployed, Wackerbarth took command of the right (Imperial Austrians, Würzburgers and Pfalz); Friesheim the centre (Walloons, Hessians and other Germans); and Bettendorf the left (Danes and Saxons). Wackerbarth would attack the woods on the western edge of the cut while the other two divisions would cross the 700m of open ground to attack the four battalions of the French Regiment du Roi deployed along the 300m of woods that formed the southern edge.

'I brought 12 guns to use against the entrenchments, but, because of the marsh, they were unable to pass quickly enough to be of use, despite the 100 fascines [bundles of brushwood] I had allocated to each battalion' (Schulenburg). It was very hard going and Schulenburg says that only seven of the original 12 guns made it through the woods.

The enemy guns opened fire when our troops approached within 700 or 800 paces of their entrenchments. [Schulenburg says that there were six French guns but French sources say five.] As my first line approached the entanglements [abatis], which were 250 paces ahead of [the main defences at the southern edge of the clearing], we sent out small groups of men to dismantle these defences and to encourage the enemy to give their first fire.

They did not fire a single shot. We were forced to tighten our line [possibly in columns to pass through gaps] quite close to the entrenchments, from which the enemy delivered a great volley, which caused disorder in our ranks as men [in the front ranks] retired.

As the terrain did not allow me to attack with all 12 battalions in the front line, I placed three battalions on the left a little to the rear to better support the first attacks. The fire of the enemy was so lively, and the defences so strong that the affair swayed back and forth for some time. Our intrepid and brave battalions were stopped short, and some were obliged to retreat five or six paces. I called up the second line, which was 200 paces behind the first, to support them. Because the enemy was trying to reoccupy the first entrenchment, from which we had driven them, and was shooting us in the flank, I also called up the third line, which was the same distance behind the second.

The fighting was fierce and bloody. Two major-generals and almost all the battalion officers were killed or wounded.

It was one of the Danish battalions on the left that first breached the main French defences. Schulenburg describes how it took two or three men of this battalion to help one man pass through the entanglements of trees and branches. 'In the end, however, they made themselves master of it, as well as six pieces of cannon that were there.'

Graf von Wackerbarth, who commanded Schulenburg's right, wrote an account 16 days after the battle. His attack was launched against the western edge of the Trieu du Bois cutting, which was held by two battalions each of the Provence, Bretagne and Saintonge regiments. In the woods, the French had constructed abatis in advance of their positions, facing north. 'They were so thin that one could pass them without too much hinderance' (Wackerbarth). The abatis were lightly held by small groups of men, who opened fire on the advancing Imperialists then withdrew to rejoin their battalions behind a more formidable barrier.

The terrain was so restrictive that in order to win it, we were forced to send out large platoons [skirmishers] in front of the battalions. As these platoons approached the entrenchments, the enemy fired a volley and then retreated behind another entrenchment also protected by abatis of more than 80 paces wide. It was behind this entrenchment that the enemy put up their greatest resistance, with the sort of effective fire one would expect from the best infantry in the world.

It took at least a quarter of an hour to pass the abatis, and it was impossible to do so in good order. As it was impossible for us to regain order, the enemy had the opportunity to adjust their fire, causing a great many casualties. We had to jump over the branches and trees as best we could, but eventually our regiments passed this abatis and gained the parapet with their bayonets and the butts of their muskets. When we gained the parapet, the enemy abandoned their positions and retreated towards their camp. (Wackerbarth)

A number of small tracks cut through the Bois de Sars, but even keeping to these, the going was very difficult. Schulenburg's men dragged 12 light guns along tracks such as this, but only seven made it through. (Author's photo)

LOTTUM'S ATTACK ON THE BOIS DE SARS, AROUND 8 A.M. (PP. 60–61)

Advancing in columns towards the French redans, Lottum's 22 battalions turned to their right to attack the south-eastern edge of the Bois de Sars. This scene captures the moment observed by de la Colonie from the French lines as Lottum's men assault the wood line, their ranks torn apart by enfilade fire from a battery of French guns.

'I could not help noticing the officer in command (**1**), who although he seemed elderly was nevertheless so active that in giving his orders there was no cessation of action anywhere, the cannon shot continued to pour forth without a break, plunged into the enemy's infantry and carried off whole ranks at a time (**2**), but a gap was no sooner created than it was immediately filled again, and they even continued their advance upon us without giving us any idea of the actual point determined on for their attack. At last the column threw itself precipitately into the wood on our left, making an assault upon that portion which had been breached.'

It was most likely Argyle's brigade that advanced on the left flank, which de la Colonie would have observed. The flag (**3**) and uniforms of the attacking troops are those of Argyle's own regiment (later the Buffs), which was one of five British battalions that took part in this attack.

The usual British fighting formation at this time was three ranks deep. First-hand descriptions of the attack speak of 'columns' rather than lines assaulting the woods. One account says that as the attackers reached the woods, they were 10–15 ranks deep.

Hidden on the edge of the wood line behind abatis, the French put up a stiff resistance. Although Lottum's men had less difficulty than Schulenburg's Imperialists, it took until 11 a.m. before they succeeded in forcing their way into the woods.

As Wackerbarth's Imperialists hacked their way through the abatis in the woods on the right, they were reinforced by Gauvin's 1,900 Hanoverians, who had marched from Mons, probably in two or three ad hoc battalions. Further to the west, Withers' 19 battalions entered the Bois de Sars from the north-west unobserved by the French. Marching in columns along the woodland tracks, they were able to pass without opposition towards the south-eastern edge of the Bois de Sars, and therefore made better progress than Wackerbarth, who had to fight his way through. This had an unintended consequence, which shall be discussed later. Meanwhile, Miklau's 20 squadrons were working their way around the far western edge of the woods to come onto the French left flank.

The corner of the Bois de Sars that was pounded by the Allied massed battery, and then attacked by Lottum's Prussians. (Author's photo)

LOTTUM'S ATTACK

As Schulenburg's men were advancing across the Trieu du Bois, the Allied grand battery of 40 guns was pummelling the corner of the woods at the south-eastern edge of the cut. The French defences of abatis and fascines greatly hindered an infantry attack, but offered no protection against a sustained artillery bombardment. The Allied shot cleared pathways through the tumble of felled trees and branches, sending wood splinters flying, increasing the casualties amongst the French defenders.

On Schulenburg's left, Lottum led his 22 battalions south towards the French redans in the open ground to the east of the Bois de Sars. Passing behind the grand battery in three columns (Argyle, Webb and Tettau/ Denhoff), it seemed as if Lottum's Prussians and British were aiming to break through the redans held by the Champagne and Irish brigades.

Holding a position in line with and to the east of the Irish Brigade, de la Colonie was able to observe Lottum's attack, and left a vivid account of it:

> They came on at a slow pace, and by seven o'clock had arrived in line with the battery threatening our centre [the 13-gun battery to Orkney's right]. As soon as this dense column appeared in the avenue, 14 guns were promptly brought up in front of our brigade almost in line with the regiment of the Gardes Françaises. The fire of this battery was terrific and hardly a shot missed its mark. I could not help noticing the officer in command who, although he seemed elderly, was nevertheless so active in giving his orders that there was no cessation of action anywhere. The cannon shot plunged into the enemy's infantry and carried off whole ranks at a time, but a gap was no

sooner created than it was immediately filled again, and they even continued their advance upon us without giving us any idea of the actual point of their attack.

At last the column, leaving the great battery on its left [the 13 guns, not the 40-gun battery], changed its direction a quarter right and threw itself precipitately into the wood on our left [the south-eastern edge of the Bois de Sars], making an assault upon that portion which had been breached [by the 40-gun battery]. It sustained the full fire of our infantry entrenched there-in and, notwithstanding the great number killed on the spot, it continued the attack and penetrated into the wood – a success which it owed as much to being drunk with brandy as to martial ardour. If all our regiments had behaved equally well, the enemy's infantry would have been entirely destroyed in this fight and would never have been able to force their way over our entrenchments.

It would seem from de la Colonie's account that Lottum's men had less difficulty than Schulenburg's. Schulenburg wrote that his men started their attack 'a little too early and even before the signal was given, which was why the troops of Count Lottum found it all the more easy to make themselves masters of the enemy entrenchments on their side'. The supporting fire from 40 guns, some of which were relatively heavy pieces, was also a huge help.

It was not, however, plain sailing. Lottum's columns had executed a very difficult manoeuvre. Under fire from the French 14-gun battery, placed by Saint-Hilaire himself, they had wheeled to the right, exposing their flank, and assaulted a fortified enemy position in woods behind a stream. Saint-Hilaire remarked: 'their manoeuvre was excellent – these people know war well'.

Mathew Bishop, a corporal in Webb's English regiment, gives a personal account of the action in which he took part:

The enemy had the advantage of the wood, which would have rendered them capable of destroying the greater part of us, had they not been intimidated [by artillery fire]. When we came near the wood, we threw all our tent poles away and ran into it as bold as lions. But we were obstructed from being so expeditious as we should by reason of their artful inventions by cutting down trees and laying them across and by tying the boughs together in all places. This they thought would frustrate us and put us into disorder. In truth, there were but very few places in that station in which we could draw up our men in any form at all. Where we did, it was in this manner – sometimes 10 deep – we were obstructed and obliged to halt, then 15 deep or more, and in this confused manner we went through the woods, but yet in high spirits.

The 'tent poles' Bishop mentions are enigmatic. One plausible interpretation offered by a modern historian (Scott) is that they were to test for boggy ground and to help them cross it, as was done at the Battle of Aughrim in 1689. It is interesting to note that Bishop says Lottum's men attacked ten deep, lending further credence to de la Colonie's descriptions of columns rather than lines.

Most modern historians say that Lottum's initial attack was repulsed, and he had to pull back to redress his ranks before making a second attempt, which was eventually successful. This contradicts de la Colonie's and Schulenburg's first-hand accounts, which say that he was able to force the

woods in the first assault. Lottum had the benefit of the supporting artillery barrage and Schulenburg's men converging on the corner of the woods from the north as he attacked from the east. This made the task somewhat easier than Schulenburg's, but possibly not so easy as to be able to take the position in a single assault.

Observing the situation from the grand battery, Marlborough rode forward to encourage Lottum's men. He reinforced them with two battalions drawn from Orkney's command in the centre (2nd Foot Guards and Orkney's battalion). Sergeant John Millner, who fought in Ingoldsby's battalion, wrote in his memoirs: 'The battalions which first attacked were entirely defeated but being sustained by fresh troops, the enemy were everywhere forced out of their entrenchments and pursued into the wood.' This account, however, could as easily be describing Schulenburg's attack as Lottum's.

At about this time, Chemerault, commanding the French redans in the centre, had assembled a force of 12 battalions to counter-attack the exposed left flank of Lottum's columns. They were probably drawn from the left redans, possibly including some of Puységur's men, who were deployed to the south of the woods. He was ready to lead them against Arglye's troops, which formed the left (southernmost) column of Lottum's attack. Marlborough anticipated the danger and ordered up 30 squadrons of d'Auvergne's Dutch horse to cover Argyle's exposed flank. Villars called a halt to the counter-attack when the Dutch squadrons advanced. 'I saw that our infantry was losing ground in the wood and I posted these 12 battalions to receive [the Allies] when they came out of it' (Villars).

By 11 a.m., Albergotti's 21 battalions had been driven from the eastern edge of the Bois de Sars. Although he had stopped Chemerault's counter-attack, Villars had sent some dragoons into the woods to dismount and hinder the Allied advance with skirmishing fire.

[The French infantry] made off for a safer quarter, leaving the position open to the enemy. As they retired, they came across the horses of the Notat Dragoons, who had been dismounted to come to their support. [The infantry] actually mounted the dragoon horses to take the better care of them while the dragoons themselves looked after the fighting business for them. (Jean-Martin de la Colonie)

THE DUTCH ATTACK

Thirty minutes after Schulenburg and Lottum began their attack on the Bois de Sars, the Dutch foot, under the overall command of the Prince of Orange, advanced towards the French entrenchments between Blairon Farm and the Bois de Lanières. French sources describe how the Dutch advanced 'with the greatest impetuosity, in five columns, towards the entrenchments on our right from the post of the Picardy Brigade to that of the Bourbonnais Brigade'.

These 'columns' were each brigades of several battalions deployed in two or three separate lines. The Prince of Orange led three on the right (Pallandt, Van Welderen and de Dohna/Van Heyden) against a protruding salient of the entrenchments defended by the Alsace Brigade. Baron Fagel led the left (Spaar/Oxenstiern and Hamilton) against the edge of the Bois de Lanières and the entrenchments to the west of the wood line.

What the Dutch did not know, until it was too late, was that the French entrenchments had been constructed to create a re-entrant, which would draw them in only to find it covered by the hidden 20-gun battery.

Despite suffering horrendous casualties from close-range fire, the Dutch reached the French entrenchments and broke through in two places. The first was on the edge of the Bois de Lanières, where the Dutch Gardes te Voet and Hamilton's Scots drove back the Comte de La Marck's regiment of Germans in French service, capturing La Marck's regimental standard.

On the right, Johan Van Pallandt's brigade of seven Dutch and Swiss battalions cleared Blairon Farm, which had not been occupied by the French, other than perhaps by skirmishers. Moving around the east of the farm, Pallandt's brigade closed on the protruding salient of the French entrenchments occupied by four battalions of the Regiment d'Alsace. After a ferocious close-quarter firefight, they succeeded in gaining the entrenchments, and forced the Alsatians to retire. The fire of the enfilade French battery, combined with musketry from the entrenchments, caused the ten battalions of Dutch and Swiss in the centre to falter.

The cost was horrendous. Within the first 30 minutes, the Dutch lost 5,000 men, with the veteran Swedish general Count Oxenstiern being one of the first, and generals Spaar and Hamilton falling later. The losses amongst the Gardes te Voet were particularly catastrophic, the second battalion suffering more than 60 per cent casualties. The French losses were also heavy. The Alsace brigade received 50 per cent casualties, and the Régiment de La Marck lost both its lieutenant-colonels and 47 officers (the number of men killed or wounded not being recorded).

Those two parts of the entrenchments, so dearly

A close-up from a mid-18th century century engraving showing the Dutch attack on the Allied left. (From *The History of England*, by Paul Rapin de Thoyras, 1740)

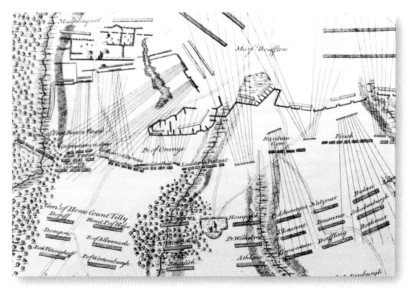

won, were soon lost to a French counter-attack. The Navarre Brigade forced back the Scots from the French right, recapturing La Marck's standard. May's Swiss brigade in French service drove the Dutch from the entrenchments they had taken from the Régiment d'Alsace.

As the Dutch foot began to fall back, Hesse-Kassel led forward his cavalry to cover their retreat and to prevent a possible French pursuit. Deputy Goslinga, who had accompanied the Prince of Orange, rode over to Major-General Rantzau, commander of the four battalions of Hanoverians just to the west of Blairon Farm. At the start of the attack, Rantzau had detached two of his battalions to join Pallandt's assault. Now, Goslinga requested the other two to reinforce the Dutch.

> Monsieur de Goslinga, passing at full gallop, came to me and asked me if I did not wish to advance. I answered that he could see quite plainly that I was advancing and that it might please him to order [Finck's] Prussians on my right to make the same movement, considering I had too little with two battalions to carry through the affair alone. Monsieur de Goslinga stopped a moment, and in his confidence of victory, or perhaps seeking to encourage the soldiers, shouted: 'La bataille est gagnée! Les braves gens!' After which he departed all the more quickly, since the enemy had forced our left to abandon the entrenchment. (Rantzau)

The Prince of Orange was not about to give up. On foot, his horse having been killed under him, he seized a flag from the Swiss regiment May in Dutch service (not to be confused with the Swiss regiment May in French service), and ran forward to plant it on the French entrenchments, encouraging his decimated troops to make a second attack. He was rejoined by Deputy Goslinga, who had two horses killed under him. It was in vain. The Dutch line wavered, and the exhausted, shell-shocked men began to fall back again. A general retreat ensued, and the Dutch foot retired to their original positions, covered by Hesse-Kassel's squadrons.

Boufflers did not pursue. Had he done so, then perhaps he could have turned the Allied left flank. It is true that Hesse-Kassel's troopers would

The view from the French enfilade battery looking east towards the Bois de Lanières. This is the view the French gunners would have had when the Dutch foot came into their sights. The small rise of the ground would have hidden the French guns from Dutch view until it was too late. (Author's photo)

THE DUTCH SECOND ATTACK, AROUND 9 A.M. (PP. 68–69)

Attacking with 30 battalions against twice that number of entrenched French infantry, supported by a battery of 20 guns, the Dutch suffered horrendous casualties. Although they succeeded in forcing the French entrenchments in two places, they lost 5,000 men in the first 30 minutes alone. A counter-attack re-established the French line, and the Dutch began to fall back.

His horse having been shot under him, the Prince of Orange (**1**) rallied his decimated troops for a second assault. He seized the flag of May's regiment (**2**), one of five Swiss regiments in Dutch service, and ran up the French earthworks to plant it on the parapet, encouraging his men to make a second attack. Some turned back (**3**), but others followed, striving to force a way over the entrenchments as the French defenders (**4**) poured fire into their ranks.

The second attack was in vain. The Dutch line wavered, and the exhausted, shell-shocked men began to fall back again. A general retreat ensued, which the French did not follow up.

The Allied cavalry advance in the centre of the battlefield. (Hulton Archive/Getty Images)

have been able to hinder pursuit, but Boufflers also had a cavalry reserve, including the elite Maison du Roi.

> Monsieur de Cebreret [commanding the Perche Brigade] came to find Maréchal de Boufflers to tell him that all his men had come out of their entrenchments, and asked to march against the enemy should he permit it, and to have them supported by the Maison du Roi and other cavalry. The Maréchal de Boufflers, in consideration of Maréchal Villars, did not wish to decide anything. There was, however, reason to believe that the Allies, shaken by their two repulsed attacks, appeared to be in disorder and could barely sustain the effort if these victorious troops were to strike their left flank. (Chevalier des Bournays, aide-de-camp to Boufflers)

The battlefield monument erected at the place where the hidden 20-gun French battery was placed on their right flank. This battery caused numerous casualties on the Prince of Orange's Dutch. (Author's photo)

Boufflers' orders were to hold the flank. Leaving the entrenchments to pursue the retreating Dutch would have far exceeded his authority without consultation with Villars. There was no time to do so. The Dutch retreat took place some time after 10 a.m. By this point, Villars' attention was firmly fixed on his left flank, where Schulenburg and Lottum were forcing d'Albergotti from the Bois de Sars.

The greatest French infantry strength was under Boufflers on the right. The overwhelming weight of the Allied attack on the Bois de Sars required some of these men to reinforce the left, but the ferocity of the Dutch attacks was such that their 30 battalions effectively pinned twice their number in place. Not only that, the Prince of

11 Septembre 1709

En ce lieu , une batterie de 20 canons du Régiment Royal Artillerie , aux ordres du Marquis de la Frézelière cause de nombreuses pertes aux troupes Hollandaises du Comte de Tilly emmenées par le Prince d'Orange et le Baron de Fagel.

Europe Mémoire Collective , Musée 1709.

ALLIED

Prince Eugene
- **A.** Gauvain (1,900 men from Mons)
- **B.** Schulenburg (40 battalions)
- **C.** Württemberg-Neuenstadt (81 squadrons)

Duke of Marlborough
- **D.** Lottum (24 battalions)
- **E.** Orkney (seven battalions)
- **F.** Finck (four battalions)
- **G.** Rantzau (two battalions)
- **H.** D'Auvergne (62 squadrons)
- **I.** Von Bülow (54 squadrons)
- **J.** Wood (15 squadrons)

Graaf van Tilly
- **K.** Orange (19 battalions)
- **L.** Fagel (13 battalions)
- **M.** Hesse-Kassel (21 squadrons)

Artillery
- **N.** 20 guns
- **O.** 28 guns
- **P.** Ten guns and three howitzers
- **Q.** 40 guns
- **R.** 12 guns

xxxxxxxxx abatis
——————— entrenchments
···················· unfinished entrenchments
⋀ ⋀ redans

BOIS DE SARS

THE INFANTRY ATTACKS,
10 A.M.–11 A.M.

EVENTS

1. Pallandt's Dutch drive the Regiment d'Alsace from the entrenchments.

2. The Dutch Guards and Scots drive back La Marck's regiment of Germans, taking the entrenchments on the French right.

3. The Prince of Orange rallies the retreating Dutch and leads them in a second assault on the French entrenchments.

4. The Navarre brigade counter-attacks to restore the French right flank.

5. May's Swiss brigade counter-attacks and drives Pallandt's Dutch from the entrenchments.

6. Marlborough orders d'Auvergne's Dutch horse forward to cover Lottum's exposed flank.

7. De la Colonie's brigade is ordered to abandon the last redans to reinforce the French counter-attack against the Bois de Sars.

8. Schulenburg and Lottum's men struggle through the woods after clearing the French abatis.

9. Reinforcements from Mons move up to support the Imperialists.

10. Detachments of dragoons move into the Bois de Sars to cover d'Albergotti's retreat.

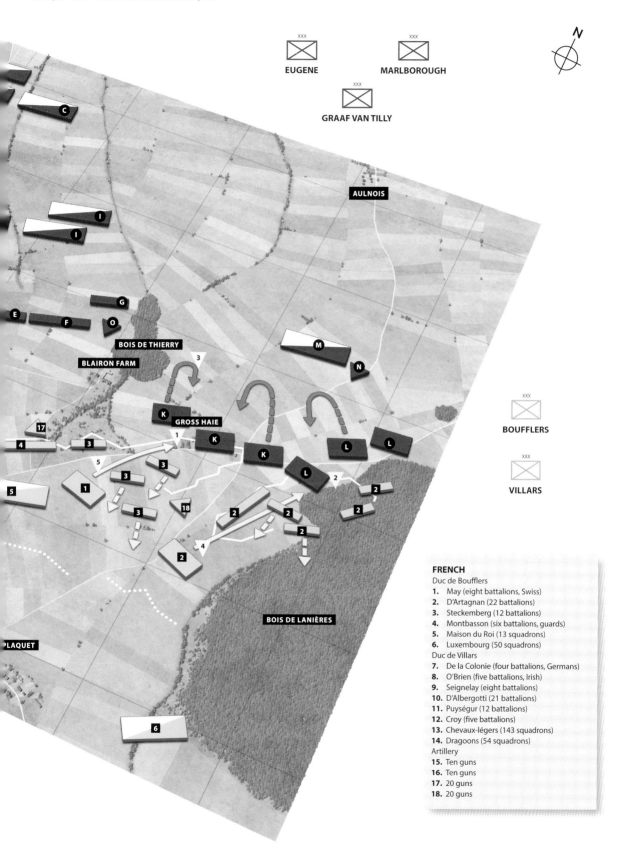

Note: gridlines are shown at intervals of 500m (547 yards)

EUGENE

MARLBOROUGH

GRAAF VAN TILLY

N

AULNOIS

BOIS DE THIERRY

BLAIRON FARM

GROSS HAIE

BOUFFLERS

VILLARS

BOIS DE LANIÈRES

LAQUET

FRENCH

Duc de Boufflers
1. May (eight battalions, Swiss)
2. D'Artagnan (22 battalions)
3. Steckemberg (12 battalions)
4. Montbasson (six battalions, guards)
5. Maison du Roi (13 squadrons)
6. Luxembourg (50 squadrons)

Duc de Villars
7. De la Colonie (four battalions, Germans)
8. O'Brien (five battalions, Irish)
9. Seignelay (eight battalions)
10. D'Albergotti (21 battalions)
11. Puységur (12 battalions)
12. Croy (five battalions)
13. Chevaux-légers (143 squadrons)
14. Dragoons (54 squadrons)

Artillery
15. Ten guns
16. Ten guns
17. 20 guns
18. 20 guns

Malplaquet church. Reconstructed in the 20th century, it was rebuilt in the same form and style as the 1709 original. (Author's photo)

Orange was reforming his decimated battalions and preparing for a third assault as the Dutch artillery engaged the French positions.

At around 10.30 a.m., Marlborough and Eugene rode over to their left, meeting with Goslinga by Rantzau's position near Blairon. Goslinga begged for further reinforcements, informing them that the Prince of Orange was preparing a third attack. The whole purpose of the Dutch attack had been to pin Boufflers' superior numbers, and this they had done at a terrific cost. Nothing more was to be gained by further casualties in an assault on a position they could not hope to take.

> The Prince [Eugene] and the Duke of Marlborough passed on their way to the left wing. Lieutenant-General Finck received from them an order for us not to quit the posts where we now were unless Mylord Duke should make us march himself. (Rantzau)

Putting a stop to a third Dutch attack, Eugene and Marlborough rode back to the centre and right, where the crisis of battle was rapidly approaching.

The Dutch attacks were almost suicidal, but they did result in completely pinning Boufflers right wing. Boufflers had to commit all his infantry reserves to hold the Dutch, and he could not spare any troops to reinforce Villars.

VILLARS' RESPONSE

By 11 a.m., the Dutch had reformed and were holding their position. Schulenburg and Lottum had broken through the French defences on the edges of the Bois de Sars, and were struggling through the woods.

> The battalions moved pell-mell. There were no generals in the centre who were able to remedy this. Everything was in great confusion, and our men suffered many casualties. Finally, we arrived at the edge of the wood overlooking the plain. There we saw the French cavalry in order of battle, and their infantry behind another entrenchment supported by said cavalry. All that was humanly possible was done to collect the battalions and form a line. (Schulenburg)

After putting a stop to another Dutch attack, Marlborough and Eugene rode over to the woods to help Schulenburg and Lottum steady their shattered battalions. They were close enough to the fighting for Eugene to be wounded by a musket ball that grazed his ear.

Villars' own observation of the confused combat in the Bois de Sars is illuminating. He describes it as 'a sort of jaws of hell, a pit of fire, sulphur and saltpetre, which it seemed impossible to approach and live'. Yet approach it the French must. This was a critical moment. If they could launch an effective counter-attack before the Allied battalions had regained their order, then the attack through the Bois de Sars could still be repulsed.

Without any hope of reinforcements from Boufflers, Villars ordered the Champagne and Irish brigades to abandon the redans and to move against the Allies who were reforming on the south-eastern edge of the woods. While the Dutch horse had prevented a previous counter-attack in the open gap, they were not a threat to an attack against the southern edge of the woods.

This garden of remembrance is maintained close to the spot where Marshal Villars was wounded. (Author's photo)

Villars' counter-attack resulted in an interesting yet puzzling encounter between a battalion of the Irish Brigade in the French army and Irish troops in the British army (Ingoldsby's battalion – later the Royal Irish).

> We happened to be the last of the regiments that had been left at Tournai to level our approaches, and therefore could not come up until all the lines were formed and closed, so there was no place for us to fall into. We were ordered, therefore, to draw up by ourselves on the right of the whole army. When the army advanced to attack the enemy, we also advanced into that part of the wood which was to our front. We continued marching slowly on, until we came to an opening in the wood. It was a small plain, on the opposite of which we perceived a battalion of the enemy drawn up. Upon this, Colonel Kane, who was then at the head of the regiment, having drawn us up and formed our platoons, advanced gently towards them with six platoons of our first fire made ready. When we had advanced within a hundred paces of them, they gave us a fire of one of their ranks, whereupon we halted and returned them the fire of our six platoons at once and immediately made ready the six platoons of our second fire and advanced upon them again. They then gave us the fire of another rank, and we returned them a second fire, which made them shrink. However, they gave us the fire of a third rank after a scattering manner, and then retired into the wood in great disorder. On which we sent our third fire after them, and saw them no more. We advanced cautiously up to the ground which they had quitted and found several of them killed and wounded; among the latter was one Lieutenant O'Sullivan, who told us that the battalion we had engaged was of the Royal Regiment of Ireland [Brigade Irlandaise]. Here, therefore, there was a fair trial of skill between the two Royal Regiments of Ireland; one in British, the other in French service … the advantage to our side will be easily accounted, for the French army carry bullets of 24 to the pound whereas our British firelocks carry 16 to the pound,

which will make a considerable difference in the execution. Again, the manner of our firing was different to theirs. The French at that time fired all by ranks, which can never do equal execution with our platoon-firing. (Captain Robert Parker)

The interesting bit is the comparison of the effects of platoon-fire versus firing by ranks. What is puzzling is that Ingoldsby's battalion was part of Withers' force, which, as Parker says, came up late from Tournai. If so, how did they end up on the left flank of the Allied troops in the Bois de Sars (south-eastern corner) to meet the French Irish, when Withers was coming from the north-west to form on the far right?

Wackerbarth, who commanded the right of Schulenburg's force, offers an explanation: 'The 19 battalions from Tournai, which were to be on my right, appeared to my left so that I held the right of the whole army.' In this case, Ingoldsby's Irish battalion would have been in a position to encounter O'Brien's Irish when they counter-attacked. Most modern historians discount Wackerbarth's account as an error. Yet Wackerbarth was there, and they were not. Furthermore, his account was written on 27 September 1709, when the events of 11 September would still have been fresh in his mind. It is not impossible to imagine how Withers' 19 battalions, marching through the woods, could have ended up further right than was originally intended. Facing no enemy opposition, they could easily have cut across the path of Wackerbarth's men, who had to fight their way through for more than three hours.

An alternative explanation is that Ingoldsby's battalion was not with Withers at all, but rather with Lottum. In favour of this is that in June 1709, the Imperial archives record Ingoldsby brigaded with Webb's battalion, which certainly fought with Lottum (see Mathew Bishop's account quoted above). This theory is partially backed up by Sergeant John Millner of Ingoldsby's battalion, who described Schulenburg and Lottum's attack (also quoted above). However, he does so as an observer, not as a participant. Furthermore, Millner also writes about the late arrival of the troops coming up from Tournai, implying that his battalion was amongst them.

Although not personally present at the battle, Parker (backed up by regimental histories) is clear that Ingoldsby's battalion was with Withers. Brigades in 1709 were temporary groupings, and their composition in June is not a reliable indication of how they were organized in September. Therefore, I am inclined to believe Wackerbarth's account as to how Ingoldsby's Irish ended up on the south-eastern edge of the Bois de Sars.

As Parker's description makes clear, the initial French counter-attack was not successful. Villars, therefore, began to look for more troops to reinforce it. He called on de la Colonie's Germans, who had occupied the redans left empty by the Irish.

By the time the Irish Brigade had got well into the wood, it was considered to be hardly sufficient as a reinforcement by itself, and an order came for us to follow it, although there was no one else left to fill our place, which would be left open to the enemy … When the first order was brought to the brigade-major, who reported it to me, I refused to obey. I pointed out the absolute necessity that existed for our maintaining the position we were holding; but a lieutenant-general then arrived on the scene and ordered us a second time to

march off, so sharply that all remonstrances were useless. (Jean Martin de la Colonie)

Although able to hold against the initial French counter-attack, the Allied generals realized that they did not have the strength to advance against Puységur's and Croy's 17 entrenched battalions supported by cavalry on the French left. Schulenburg recounts that the seven guns he had managed to drag through the woods proved to be of great use. The French had no artillery on their left flank, and so Schulenburg's battery was able to engage the French positions without them being able to respond.

The French, Irish and German battalions taken from the redans were not sufficient to dislodge Lottum, Schulenburg and Withers from the woods, so, at around noon, Villars rallied the survivors of d'Albergotti's men to join them, and probably also called up Puységur's reserve to form a force of 50 battalions for a more concerted counter-attack. At that moment, Villars was shot in the knee and forced to retire from the field. Chemerault was killed at the same time, and d'Albergotti wounded shortly afterwards. This sudden removal of the key general officers stopped the attack from going ahead.

> One shot and my horse fell. I jumped up and a second broke my knee. I had it bandaged on the spot and myself placed in a chair to continue giving orders. But the pain caused a fainting fit, which lasted long enough for me to be carried off without regaining consciousness. That is all I know about the end of the battle. (Villars)

The French active defence on their left suddenly ground to a halt, as brigade commanders had to make their own decisions without the benefit of higher-level coordinated command. 'Each brigade fought, as it were, independently, without being in the least aware of its neighbours' movements' (Jean-Martin de la Colonie). Command of the French left fell to Puységur, who was either not inclined, or unable, to coordinate and execute Villars' planned counter-attack.

Boufflers now had overall command of the army, but he was on the far right and pinned by the ferocity of the previous Dutch attacks. Although Marlborough had prevented a third Dutch attack, Boufflers did not know this, and the Dutch infantry, supported by horse, had reformed and still threatened the French right.

Villars had been forced to abandon the redans in the centre to find troops to counter-attack the Allies in the Bois de Sars. This did not go unnoticed by Marlborough, who, at noon, was forward with Schulenburg. Schulenburg recounts that he told Marlborough the redans had been abandoned, and urged him to occupy them without delay. Marlborough rode back to the centre. When a scouting party of Imperial hussars confirmed that the redans were indeed empty of French infantry, Marlborough ordered Orkney, Finck and Rantzau's British, Prussians and Hanoverians forward to capture them.

THE CAVALRY BATTLE

Although the redans were empty, the entrenchments to their immediate right (east) were occupied by six battalions of the elite Gardes Suisses and Gardes Françaises. Boufflers had ordered the guards to extend their line to the west to partially fill the gap in the French centre. They were the only opposition the Allies faced, and they did not live up to their elite reputation, as de la Colonie scathingly recounts:

> When [the Allied] battalions advanced to seize our entrenchments, the fine infantry [the guards] holding our centre who had so far not suffered from a single hostile shot, had every opportunity of deploying to cover the gap made by our empty entrenchments, but then they would have run still more the risk of spoiling their beautiful uniforms, their most noticeable characteristic. Therefore, they retired to try and find a quieter spot, where they would be safe from any such rough handling.

By 1 p.m., the Allied foot had occupied the French redans, and Marlborough ordered the cavalry of d'Auvergne, Wood and von Bülow to advance and pass through them to attack the French horse drawn up behind. He also called on Hesse-Kassel to move over to the centre from his position supporting the Dutch on the left. Württemberg's Danish and Imperial squadrons followed up behind.

The Allied horse had to this point suffered no casualties. The French, however, had been subjected to a constant bombardment from the Allied artillery, suffering especially from the indirect fire of the howitzers deployed to Orkney's right. The Marquis de la Frézelière reported seeing three 'bombs' from the howitzers exploding in quick succession amongst the same squadron. Some modern historians say that Marlborough repositioned his 40-gun grand battery to fire on the French horse in the centre after they could no longer support Lottum's attack. This is highly unlikely. Walking the battlefield, it is clear that, from their original position, the gunners could not have seen any targets. It would have been impossible to call up the civilian limber teams and the vast number of horses needed to move the heavy guns forward while the battle was still raging. With 30 guns and three howitzers deployed in line with Orkney, there was plenty of ordnance to severely damage the French horse.

As the Allied cavalry passed through the redans, the French horse moved forward to meet them. It was the largest cavalry battle of the age, with 30,000 Allied troopers advancing to meet almost the same number of French. Boufflers himself joined the Maison du Roi to lead their charge. The first Allied squadrons were thrown back, but the French were not able to pursue, thanks to covering fire from the Allied infantry who had occupied the redans.

The action flowed back and forth to the south of the redans, the French horse charging six times to drive the enemy back. An account in the Dutch archives reports that 'both sides broke on various occasions, but finally, the enemy, always finding the fire of our infantry in its path, seriously considered retreating'.

Peter Drake, an Irishman serving in the ranks of the French Gendarmes, gives an interesting account of the cavalry action in which he took part:

This contemporary painting by Jan van Huchtenburg captures a sense of the ferocity of the cavalry combat in the centre at Malplaquet. The background bears no resemblance to the actual battlefield. (Zip Lexing/Alamy)

> Sixty-three squadrons of the French horse; the Maison du Roi and Gendarmes being part of that number to the amount of 21 squadrons; all of which were ordered to march down to engage a large body of the enemy's horse, who had

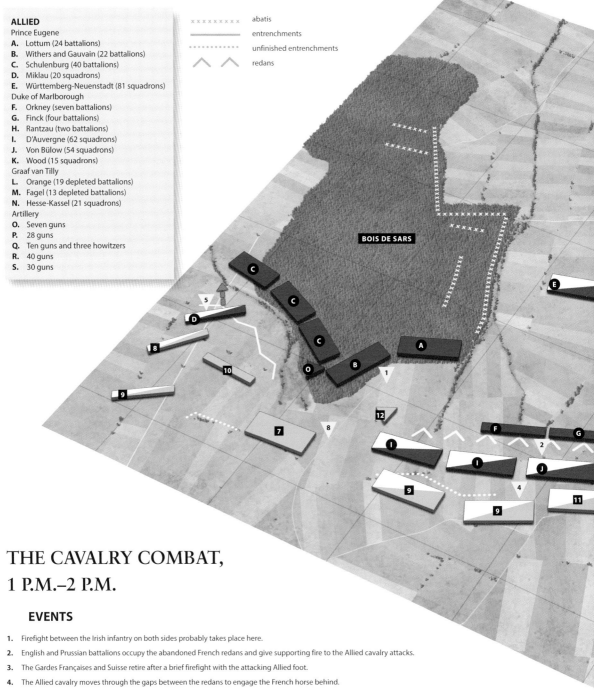

x x x x x x x x   abatis
———————   entrenchments
. . . .   unfinished entrenchments
∧ ∧   redans

BOIS DE SARS

THE CAVALRY COMBAT, 1 P.M.–2 P.M.

EVENTS

1. Firefight between the Irish infantry on both sides probably takes place here.

2. English and Prussian battalions occupy the abandoned French redans and give supporting fire to the Allied cavalry attacks.

3. The Gardes Françaises and Suisse retire after a brief firefight with the attacking Allied foot.

4. The Allied cavalry moves through the gaps between the redans to engage the French horse behind.

5. French carabiniers drive off Miklau's flanking cavalry.

6. The survivors of the Dutch attack recover their order and prepare for a third assault.

7. Hesse-Kassel's Dutch cavalry are ordered over to the centre to reinforce the Allied cavalry attack.

8. Villars is severely wounded while gathering together 50 battalions to counter-attack the Bois de Sars. The counter-attack does not take place.

Note: gridlines are shown at intervals of 500m (547 yards)

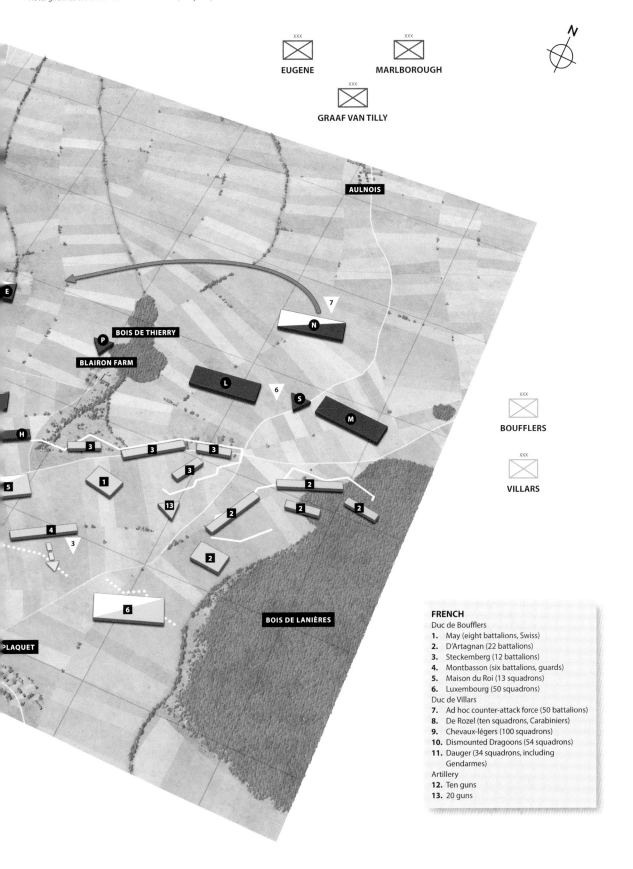

EUGENE

MARLBOROUGH

GRAAF VAN TILLY

N

AULNOIS

7

N

BOIS DE THIERRY

P

BLAIRON FARM

L

6

S

M

BOUFFLERS

H

3

3

3

VILLARS

1

3

5

2

13

2

2

2

4

3

2

6

BOIS DE LANIÈRES

PLAQUET

FRENCH
Duc de Boufflers
1. May (eight battalions, Swiss)
2. D'Artagnan (22 battalions)
3. Steckemberg (12 battalions)
4. Montbasson (six battalions, guards)
5. Maison du Roi (13 squadrons)
6. Luxembourg (50 squadrons)
Duc de Villars
7. Ad hoc counter-attack force (50 battalions)
8. De Rozel (ten squadrons, Carabiniers)
9. Chevaux-légers (100 squadrons)
10. Dismounted Dragoons (54 squadrons)
11. Dauger (34 squadrons, including
    Gendarmes)
Artillery
12. Ten guns
13. 20 guns

already got within our entrenchments that were made between the two woods … The squadron that I belonged to was commanded by the Chevalier de Janson … who ordered that six men on the right and six men on the left of his squadron should, on a signal given by him, detach themselves and fall on the flanks of the squadron we should engage, and pour in their carbine shot among them, whilst he would, with the remainder of the squadron sword in hand, endeavour to break through the enemy.

This had the desired effect. We had to do with Germans, and by this stratagem we broke through them and through a second by the like method … We marched on to engage a third squadron, which broke in seeming confusion, or rather opened right and left on purpose to draw us under the fire of Colonel Pendergast's [British infantry] regiment, who lay unseen by us at the reverse of the entrenchment and poured their shot amongst us, and some other French squadrons that had penetrated so far, which made a great slaughter.

Drake's account shows us how the French horse used firepower as well as charging home with swords to great effect. He also emphasises the decisive impact of the Allied supporting infantry preventing the French horse from following up any successes. Orkney himself recounted: 'I really believe had not the foot been there, [the French cavalry] would have driven our horse from the field.'

As the cavalry battle was raging in the centre, another one developed on the French left. Miklau's 20 squadrons had made their way around the western edge of the Bois de Sars, and had emerged by the hamlet of La Folie. The arrival of 20 squadrons on the French left may have helped to turn that flank, had Withers, Schulenburg and Lottum been able to launch an attack from their positions on the southern edge of the Bois de Sars; but they were too exhausted from the fierce fighting in the woods to attack the fresh, entrenched French infantry facing them.

This Dutch print depicts the cavalry combat that took place after the French abandoned their redans in the centre. (Jan van Huchtenburg)

The French had substantial cavalry reserves on the left able to counter Miklau, who was isolated and unsupported. The Chevalier de Rozel led forward ten squadrons of the elite French Carabiniers to take Miklau's cavalry as they were forming up. A few days earlier, the Carabiniers had suffered in a skirmish at the hands of Imperial hussars, and as a result gave no quarter. 'Almost all the officers of the enemy's right were killed or captured. One has never seen such carnage in a cavalry action. We followed them into the woods and took from them their standards' (de Rozel).

This early 20th-century painting gives a romanticized depiction of the French carabiniers (blue uniforms) charging Miklau's Imperialist cavalry. The uniform details are not correct. (Painting by Richard Simkin)

THE FRENCH RETREAT

By 2 p.m., the cavalry action in the centre had ground to a standstill. The French horse had the better of the engagements, but they could make no headway while the Allied foot occupied the redans. The Allies were masters of the Bois de Sars, and, although they had not debouched from the woods, they had recovered their order and vastly outnumbered the French on that wing.

Schulenburg is clear in his memoirs that he saw no possibility of success if he was to advance against Puységur, now reinforced by the French, Irish and German troops drawn from the centre. Some modern historians imagine that Withers did, perhaps, come out of the woods to move on Puységur's left flank, but this is not backed up by any primary accounts. If we believe, as I do, that Wackerbarth is correct, and that Withers ended up more to the east (explaining the combat between the two Irish battalions), then he would not have been in any position to do so.

Puységur, finding himself unexpectedly in command of the French left, took stock of the situation. The moment for an effective counter-attack on that flank had passed. The Allied foot, outnumbering him, had reformed on

THE CAVALRY ACTION, AROUND 2 P.M. (PP. 84–85)

Villars stripped his infantry from the redans in the centre of the battlefield to counter-attack the Bois de Sars on the French left. Marlborough sent Orkney and Finck's infantry forward to occupy the abandoned fortifications, and then ordered his cavalry to attack. Passing through the gaps between the redans, they engaged the French cavalry stationed behind them. A huge cavalry battle ensued, which flowed back and forth. The French initially had the upper hand, but were unable to exploit their success due to fire from the British and Prussian infantry who now occupied the redans.

The elite French Gendarmes came up against von Bülow's Prussians and Hanoverians. Irishman Peter Drake was serving with the Gendarmes Anglais. He became separated from his troop when they came under fire from British infantry in the redans, and found himself confronted by some of Von Bülow's men. He gives a first-hand account of the action:

'I approached the German officer (**1**). He had a pistol cocked in his hand, aiming the muzzle of his pistol at my right shoulder and

firing. I fired my carbine at the same time (**2**) so that his shot and mine went off instantaneously. I shot the upper part of his head and he tumbled forward. I saw his brains come down. His ball only grazed my shoulder and tore the flesh a little. But the powder blew off and burnt my coat (**3**). The wadding lodged between my waistcoat and shirt, setting them both on fire. His squadron fired a volley at the same time so that I had 11 shot fairly marked on my cuirass and two through the skirts of my coat.'

This evocative account is typical of close-quarter mounted action at a time when firearms were still often used in preference to swords.

We do not know which unit Peter Drake encountered. They are depicted as von Bülow's Hanoverian dragoons. Drake wears the red, silver-trimmed uniform of the Gendarmes. His bandolier (**4**) and the cypher on his pistol holders (**5**) were distinctive of the Gendarmes Anglais, recruited primarily from men with Jacobite sympathies from the British Isles.

A battlefield monument commemorating the French carabiniers' victory over Miklau's Imperialists. (Author's photo)

the edge of the Bois de Sars, and were potentially poised to attack. Although Miklau's flanking cavalry had been driven off, he could see that the Allied horse to his right had breached the redans. He risked being outflanked and annihilated if he remained in place, so he began to make preparations to withdraw.

Boufflers was personally leading the French cavalry attacks in the centre, and therefore did not have an overview of what was happening elsewhere. It may have been the case that Puységur began an orderly withdrawal without direct orders. Then, as the cavalry battle ground down to a stalemate, Boufflers began to realize that he could not hope to hold the field of battle.

On their right flank the French still had advantage of numbers, but Boufflers had not launched a counter-attack on the Dutch when they first fell back, and now it was too late, as the Dutch had begun to move forward yet again, as Prince Eugene recounts: 'As at the beginning of the battle, so now the Dutch bought with their blood every step of the broad earth. In the end, the French right wing had to abandon the field to such death-defying courage.'

At around 3 p.m., Boufflers ordered the army to retire from the field, despite the fact that the French had suffered far fewer casualties than the Allies. This order was met with dismay by many French officers and men, especially those on the right. 'Why did we retire? We have beaten them and forced all the enemy who attacked us to retire … we were very angry and very sad' (Chevalier de Quincy, recounting the feelings of those on the French right).

The French left the field in good order, taking 66 of their 80 guns with them. This was no mean feat in an era when the relative immobility of artillery tended to result in a retreating army losing most of its ordinance to the enemy. The Allies, however, were in no position to pursue. They had suffered horrendous casualties, and the French were able to conduct an organized retirement, covered by their still substantial reserves of horse.

A tapestry from Blenheim Palace showing Marlborough dispatching a rider with orders. In the background, the English, Prussians and Hanoverians are advancing on the French centre. (The Picture Art Collection/Alamy)

Europe at the end of the War of the Spanish Succession

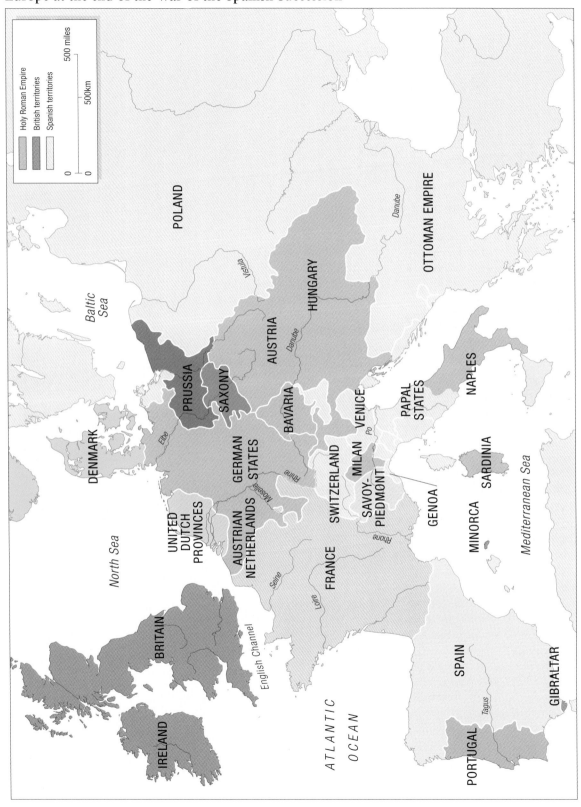

Holy Roman Empire
British territories
Spanish territories

500 miles
500km

POLAND

Vistula

OTTOMAN EMPIRE

Danube

HUNGARY

Baltic Sea

AUSTRIA

Danube

PRUSSIA

SAXONY

BAVARIA

VENICE

PAPAL STATES

NAPLES

DENMARK

Elbe

GERMAN STATES

Rhine

SWITZERLAND

MILAN

Po

SARDINIA

Mediterranean Sea

Moselle

SAVOY-PIEDMONT

GENOA

MINORCA

UNITED DUTCH PROVINCES

AUSTRIAN NETHERLANDS

Seine

FRANCE

Loire

Rhone

North Sea

BRITAIN

English Channel

SPAIN

GIBRALTAR

ATLANTIC OCEAN

IRELAND

Tagus

PORTUGAL

AFTERMATH

So, who won the battle?

The French achieved their strategic aim. They had prevented an invasion of France. Although they had quit the field, their army was still in good order. The slaughter of Allied troops turned the strategic situation of early 1709 on its head. Then, the confident Allies had rebuffed Louis XIV's peace overtures. Now, the Dutch, British and Imperial courts began to desperately seek a way out of the costly conflict. The Battle of Malplaquet changed the course of the war. It led indirectly to Marlborough's eventual dismissal, and peace settlements in 1713 and 1714 that were far more favourable to the French than the terms Louis had offered in early 1709.

An immediate consequence of the battle was that the French army regained its heart. Reviewing the army on 16 September, Boufflers wrote: 'It is more beautiful and proud than before the battle.' A number of Allied participants expressed similar sentiments: 'Although the enemy lost the field, they recovered a part of their former reputation by standing the attack so boldly as they then did' (Sergeant John Millner).

This scene of French soldiers at Valenciennes was painted in 1710. Valenciennes was one of the towns the French army fell back on after the battle. (Jean-Antoine Watteau)

The Allies, on the other hand, lost the confidence they had enjoyed after their victories of 1708, and recriminations followed. The Dutch were particularly aggrieved at the scale of their casualties. They lost 9,000 men, compared to 1,800 British. Accusations were levelled at Marlborough that he had deliberately sacrificed the Dutch to save British lives. The Prince of Orange complained that if Withers' force had been sent to reinforce him, as originally intended, then he would have had sufficient troops to win on his flank. Some British and Austrian commentators countered this by alleging that the prince had

The valiant French defence at Malplaquet secured Villars' reputation as the saviour of the nation. This painting shows Villars leading the French to victory over Eugene at Denain in 1712. (GL Archive/Alamy)

After Malplaquet the Allies pressed the siege of Mons, as this print commemorates. (Anne S.K. Brown Military Collection)

exceeded his orders and continued his attacks with recklessness, when he should merely have been conducting a diversionary attack. None of the accusations from either quarter are really justified, although it is easy to see how the various Allied participants would have felt aggrieved.

It is not unreasonable, therefore, to say that Malplaquet was actually a French victory of sorts. It was certainly a strategic victory, if not a tactical one. If so, it was probably the French cavalry that saved the day. Given the strength of the French position, Marlborough's plan was a good one, and it worked reasonably well. The attacks on the flanks fixed the French infantry and caused Villars to weaken his centre. This gave an opening that Marlborough exploited. Had the Allied cavalry managed to break through the centre, the French army would probably have been routed.

Overcoming the humiliations of Blenheim and Ramillies, the French horse managed to throw back the 30,000 Dutch, German and British troopers sent against them – this despite having endured a seven-hour artillery bombardment. This prevented an Allied breakthrough in the centre, and allowed the orderly retreat of the French army. The close coordination of horse and foot was a hallmark of Marlborough's battles, and was certainly a feature at Malplaquet. Had it not been for the Allied infantry's occupation of the abandoned redans, the French horse may well have been able to break the Allied centre.

Malplaquet was the first European battle in which artillery played such a key role. Both sides deployed massed batteries at key points, coordinated with the other arms. The grand 40-gun battery that supported Lottum's attack, and the enfilading 20 French guns that decimated the Dutch, were both crucial to the success of their respective wings. Such artillery tactics became the norm in later years, but in 1709 they were quite revolutionary.

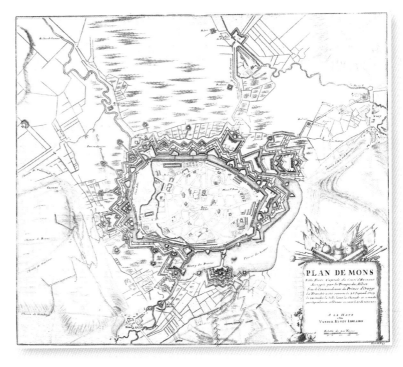

A contemporary plan of Mons in 1709. The town fell on 20 October. (Engraving by Pieter van Call)

Some later French historians have suggested that Villars might have won outright, had he not entrenched so many of his infantry on the right. Fighting from entrenchments fixed the French foot in place, discouraging Boufflers from counter-attacking the Dutch and making it difficult to move men from the right to the hard-pressed left.

The French army retired from the field of battle in good order, and the Allies were in no condition to pursue. Marlborough and Eugene fell back to Blaregnies, while Boufflers dispersed the French army to reinforce the towns and fortresses along the French frontier. He even managed to slip three battalions through the Allied lines to reinforce the garrison of Mons.

Having failed to break through into France, the Allies turned their attention back to Mons, which was defended by 4,280 (mostly Spanish) troops under the command of the Marquis de Grimaldi. Boufflers received orders from the king not to risk another battle, and, therefore, he made no attempt to relieve Mons. Grimaldi held out until 20 October, conducting an active defence that resulted in 2,000 Allied casualties to his 700.

By the time Mons fell, it was too late in the season for any more campaigning, so the Allied armies dispersed into winter quarters. In early 1709, they had been confident that they could break the French. After Malplaquet, they had taken Tournai and Mons, but the French army was not only undefeated, it had also regained a new confidence. In a letter to his king, Villars encapsulated the situation: 'If God give us grace to lose such another battle, your majesty may reckon that your enemies are annihilated.'

The Battle of Malplaquet did not end the war, but it did eventually lead to an outcome that was far more favourable to the French than Louis XIV could possibly have hoped for when he first sued for peace in the spring of 1709. As such it must be regarded as one of the most decisive battles of the War of Spanish Succession despite its relatively inconclusive outcome on the day.

THE BATTLEFIELD TODAY

Unusually for an 18th-century European battlefield, Malplaquet is reasonably well signposted.

Just south of the French-Belgian border there is a monument commemorating the battle. This should be the first stop for any visitor. Surrounding the monument, with its acknowledgements to the French, British, Dutch and German participants, are a number of excellent battlefield maps set up for the 300th anniversary of the battle in 2009.

The detail on the maps is incredibly accurate, thanks to the efforts of the local French aristocrat Arthur Barbera, who devoted much of his life to studying the battle. Unfortunately, Barbera died in 2012, and the battlefield museum he once maintained in Bavay is now closed. There are rumours that it may reopen in Taisnières-sur-Hon, but at time of writing, this has not yet happened.

There is nothing on the Belgian side of the border to note the original Allied positions, but on the French side there are a number of stations marked

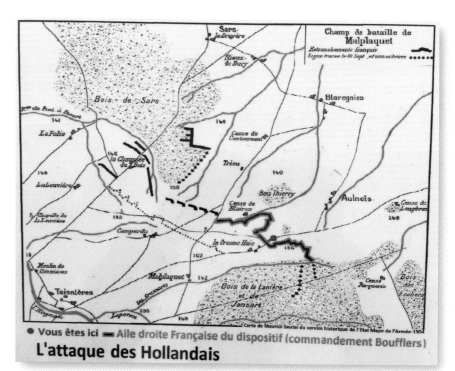

One of the many battlefield signs that orients the visitor and explains the view. (Author's photo)

with memorials and maps. At each point, the visitor is presented with a monument or signpost that explains where a significant event happened, backed up by maps.

Mons makes a suitable base for exploring, as the battlefield is only 10km to the south. To visit, you need a car. Although the distances are not great, there is no public transport servicing the area. Parking your car at the monument, you can easily tramp over most of the battlefield on foot. You can then take your car to explore the further reaches, such as the site of the French enfilade battery to the east (marked by a monument) or La Folie and the site of the cavalry action between de Rozel and Miklau to the west (also marked by a monument). A 15km walking tour – the Circuit Malbrouck – is signposted. Its starting point is the Belgian village of Blaregnies, which was the centre of the Allied camp both before and after the battle.

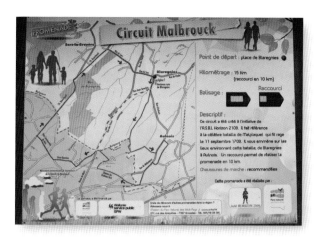

A 15km walking circuit, starting at Blaregnies, encompasses the entire battlefield. (Author's photo)

The battlefield monument stands between the French and Allied lines on the side of the road from Mons to Malplaquet. It is the best place to start a tour, thanks to the excellent maps placed there. (Author's photo)

The intervening centuries have left no trace of the redans or entrenchments dug by the French in 1709. Malplaquet was on the route of the British retreat from Mons in 1914, and has now gone back to agricultural land. It is, however, possible to walk the battlefield and gain a sense of the terrain fought over more than 300 years ago. The outline of the Bois de Sars (today known as the Bois de Blaregnies) is more or less as it was on 11 September 1709. It is still possible to contemplate the difficulty Schulenburg and Lottum must have experienced as they forced their way through the dense woods. Although the Bois de Thierry has disappeared, Blairon Farm (today usually written Bléron) still stands. A walk alongside the stream that runs beside it gives some idea of the nearly impenetrable barrier it must have caused.

Walking the battlefield, it becomes immediately obvious just how limited fields of fire must have been. Although the gap is still relatively open and flat, there are very few occasions where visibility to a man on foot exceeds 200m. There are no hills or ridges, but the small folds in the ground hinder visibility much more than one would assume from a glance on a topographical map.

Although further away than Mons, Tournai offers another possible base to explore the battlefield, especially if one wishes to take in more of the whole campaign. Almost nothing remains of Tournai's 18th-century defences, thanks in part to the efforts of the Luftwaffe in 1940 and RAF in 1944. There is, however, an excellent little military museum that tells the story of the city at war from Roman times to World War II.

FURTHER READING

Belloc, Hilaire, *British Battles – Malplaquet*, Stephen Swift & Co., London, 1911

Chandler, David, *Marlborough as a Military Commander*, Military Book Society, 1973

Chartrand, René, *Louis XIV's Army* (Men-at-Arms 203), Osprey Pubishing Ltd., London, 1988

Churchill, Winston, *Marlborough: His Life and Times*, vol. 2, Charles Scribner's Sons, London, 1947

Coxe, William, and Wade, John, *Memoirs of John, Duke of Marlborough*, vol 2, G. Bell and Sons, London, 1847

De la Colonie, Jean-Martin, *The Chronicles of an Old Campaigner, 1692–1717*, Forgotten Books, London, 2015

Drake, Peter, *Amiable Renegade: The Memoirs of Captain Peter Drake 1671–1753*, Oxford University Press, Oxford, 1960

Falkner, James, *Marlborough's Battlefields*, Pen & Sword, Barnsley, 2008

Goldberg, Claus-Peter, *Deutsche Staaten*, CD-Rom, Baccus 6MM, 1993

Hall, Robert, Boeri, Giancarlo, and Roumegoux, Yves, *French Cavalry under Louis XIV 1688–1714*, CD-Rom, Baccus 6MM, 2005

Hall, Robert, and Boeri, Giancarlo, *Uniforms and Flags of the Imperial Austrian Army 1683–1720*, CD-Rom, Baccus 6MM, 2008

Hall, Robert, Roumegoux, Yves, and Stanford, Iain, *Uniforms and Flags of the Dutch Army and the Army of Liege 1685–1715*, CD-Rom, Baccus 6MM, 2013

Kearsey, A., *Marlborough and his Campaigns, 1702–1709*, Gale and Polden, Aldershot, 1929

Kühn, August (revised by Robert Hall), *Brandenburg–Prussia's Army under King Frederick I*, CD-Rom, Baccus 6MM, 2001

Ligne, Charles Joseph (trans. William Mudford), *Memoirs of Prince Eugene of Savoy*, Sherwood, Neely, and Jones, London, 1811

Maycock, F. W. O., *An Outline of Marlborough's Campaigns*, Pallas Armata, Tonbridge, 1992

Millner, John, *A Compendious Journal of all the Marches, Famous Battles and Sieges 1701–1712*, Naval and Military Press, Uckfield, 2004

Nosworthy, Brent, *The Anatomy of Victory*, Hippocrene Books, New York, 1992

Sautai, Maurice (trans. G. F. Nafziger), *The Battle of Malplaquet*, The Nafziger Collection, West Chester, 2007

Scott, Christopher, *Malplaquet 1709*, Partizan Press, Eastwood, 2009

INDEX

Figures in **bold** refer to illustrations.